DYING FOR ACTION

DYING FOR ACTION
THE LIFE AND FILMS OF JACKIE CHAN

Renée Witterstaetter

WARNER BOOKS

A Time Warner Company

*This book is dedicated to my mother, Erma, and to my late father,
Raymond, who not only brought me into this world, but performed their own amazing
stunts and heroic acts to send me out to discover it unafraid.*

Photographs courtesy of Media Asia Group. Copyright STAR TV.

Copyright © 1997 by Renée Witterstaetter
All rights reserved.

Warner Books, Inc., 1271 Avenue of the Americas, New York, NY 10020

Visit our Web site at
http://warnerbooks.com

W A Time Warner Company

Printed in the United States of America
First Printing: October 1997
10 9 8 7 6 5 4 3 2 1
Library of Congress Cataloging-in-Publication Data
Witterstaetter, Renee.
    Dying for action : the life and films of Jackie Chan / Renee Witterstaetter.
        p.   cm.
    Includes bibliographical references.
    ISBN 0-446-67296-3
    1. Ch' eng, Lung, 1955– . I. Title.
PN2878.C52W58   1997
791.43'028'092—dc21
    [B]   97-1866
                                                              CIP

Book design and text composition by H. Roberts
Cover design by Janet Perr
Cover photo of Lightning courtesy of Liason International/Gone Peach
Cover photo Jackie Chan courtesy of Media Asia Group. © STAR TV

Acknowledgments

- **Special thanks to** friend and colleague Ric Meyers, and to my agent, Don Maass, and to my family. Thanks also to my editors, Wayne Chang and Betsy Mitchell, as well as to Jim Salicrup; Michael Golden; Caroline Vie; Charlie Chan; Solon So and Davis Fung of the JC Group; Joy Al-Sofi, Richard Cooper and Christine Mullen, fan club presidents; Mars; Ken Lo; the Jackie Chan stuntmen; Edward Tang; Fong; Papa Chan; Christina Nathanail; Osumi; Russell Cawthorne of Golden Harvest; Nicholas James and Bey Logan of Media Asia; David Imhoff of New Line Cinema; Steve Bunche; Marie Javins, who took me to my first JC movie; Tim Prickett, who always said I could; Dr. Laurence McNamee, for his support; Gertrude Cozad and Maureen VanDerStad, for their guidance; Mariah Aquilar; Joan Hershy at *A&E Biography*; fan supreme Seaton Chiang; F. J. DeSanto of BatFilm; Louis Roth; Vincent Lynn; Peter Chow; the defunct Sun Sing Theater; the Miramax/Dimension junket crew; the New Line junket crew; Web site wiz Mike Mikaelian; and computer guru Brian Boerner. All of these people in some way have been either kind, helpful or enthusiastic—many of them all of the above.

- **Most special thanks** is reserved for Jackie Chan and Willie Chan.

Contents

*"Making a movie, I'm not scared. I can die for the movie.
I don't want to die for nothing."*

—Jackie Chan
February 1996

FOREWORD

—OR—

THE DAY JACKIE CHAN BEAT RAGING BULL

IT CANNOT BE EXAGGERATED how big a star Jackie Chan is in most parts of the world. To say he has the fan following of Arnold Schwarzenegger, Sylvester Stallone, Bruce Willis, Jean-Claude Van Damme and Buster Keaton combined borders on just about right. To say his talent meets and exceeds the output of all these men is subjective, but still arguable.

He's been there, and not only done "that," but done it all—from comedy, action and drama to period films and death-defying stunts.

For years, this Hong Kong actor has unassumingly been building a fan following in the United States—a devoted corps of action movie lovers searching doggedly for bootleg tapes of Chan's films to fill their insatiable hunger for the incredible.

Now their search will be much easier.

After twenty years as the top action star in the world, Jackie Chan has begun his assault on America in earnest. Many of you may only remember him from such poor vintage vehicles as *Cannonball Run* or *The Protector*. Many more of you may have just been introduced to Chan via New Line's *Rumble in the Bronx* or Miramax's *Police Story*—both revitalized Hong Kong imports. You'll doubtless be seeing more of Chan in movies to come, both revamped oldies-but-goodies and new efforts.

The first time I saw Jackie Chan, believe it or not, he was sitting quite still.

The year was 1992, Hong Kong, and I'd just arrived on the set of one of the two movies he was filming at that time—*Crime Story* (*Supercop* being the other)—to see the actor at work and gather information for a comic book I wanted to produce, an idea that had come to me after seeing one of Jackie's movies by chance in New York.

Little did I know that, within two weeks of allowing a friend to persuade me to see a Hong Kong movie by some guy named Chan instead of renting *Raging Bull*, I'd be on a plane to Asia and then stepping foot onto a movie set with that same actor. Yet here I was. And there Jackie *sat* reading a paper.

I was soon to learn that that would be one of the few times I would see Mr. Chan at rest, as over the next few weeks I watched Jackie run down busy streets, jump over barricades, vault off a truck, give better than he got while sparring with the Chinese military and throw me into a scene or two with his personal direction, coaching me in the art of acting for film (or at least drinking a cup of coffee—my demanding role).

I returned home, eventually, with one truth: Nobody loves making movies more than Chan; nobody is more willing to give his all for the audiences like Chan; nobody is *dying* for action like Jackie Chan. Whether or not you agree with his tactics and his flirtation with the risky, it's indisputable that Jackie Chan is a juggernaut of creativity.

Actually, his every film is a continuation of his autobiography—the ballet of the human body as performed by Jackie Chan. There are glimpses into his life and opinions in every movie he makes—not to mention a chronological account of every broken bone and crushed head, broken finger and twisted knee.

Out of respect for Jackie, I must say that this is not a tell-all book about his life. If that's ever to be written, Jackie will have to do it himself. He's the only one who has been there. However, in this book we will touch upon all of Jackie's major movies, talk about what makes them "major" and include behind-the-scenes sidebars and descriptions of his showstopper fights and stunts.

So, action movie lovers, martial arts fans and students, readers of the Topps Comics Jackie Chan series, those discovering Hong Kong cinema for the first time—this book serves as your companion. Pick it up and have fun.

Jackie Chan, for his whole career, may have been dying for action, dying for the next adrenaline-pumping jump. But, as he starts a new chapter in his story, he's also dying for *you* to discover him.

R.W.
New York, 1996

IX

CHAN: TAKE TWO

"ALL OF AMERICA LOVES JACKIE CHAN—They Just Don't Know It Yet," the sign reads, clutched proudly by a fan in a crowd of twenty-five, waiting for their hero to arrive at the Los Angeles airport. He is coming to America . . . again . . . this time to promote his latest film, *Rumble in the Bronx*.

He has been here before. Only then . . . there had been no crowd.

Jackie Chan, an effervescent, stunt-crazy action star from Hong Kong, has his Beatles mop-top of a coif commented on because of the way, when he's kicked or jumps off a building, it defies gravity—much like the rest of his body in his forty-odd movies as the leading action star in the world. That hair isn't the only resemblance to the Fab Four. He too has experienced the raw thrill, *and* terror, of the adoring mob rushing—the fans with their "love" crushing up against his van, in search of a scribbled signature to press somewhere and tell people years from now that "they remember when . . ." He has seen the obsessed commit suicide when his private life is reported—one girl drank poison in front of his office building and another threw herself in front of a train for unrequited love. He has had the feeling of not really knowing what a normal life might be. After all, he's never had one.

Just how big is Jackie Chan in most parts of the world? Is there a contrast to the Beatles? Well, unlike Lennon, he's never claimed to be bigger than Jesus Christ . . . even though they *do* share the same initials.

Here, at the L.A. airport in 1996, Chan reasons, based on previous trips to the United States, that he will not face any fans who will hound him through airports or chase him through busy streets in taxis like they do in Japan, Thailand or Korea. Today, all of that exists in other countries. Not here . . . not in *America*. He has wooed this lady before. She will never accept his gung-ho style of filmmaking and sense of humor, he thinks.

She is the last holdout in his world bid for love.

Yet, as he disembarks and smiles at the modest—by his standards—welcoming committee, he has his first inkling that this time things will be different. Now the fans *are* here.

Flashback to 1980 and Jackie's first attempt at American stardom: Chan may have been able to know what it was like to walk down the street like everybody else—something for which he claims to occasionally yearn. Only he didn't want it then. He wanted to jump and somersault and say, "Look at me. I'm here, America. Love me." Raymond Chow, head of Golden Harvest in Hong Kong, was trying to give Chan that chance. After successes like *Drunken Master* (1978) and *Young Master* (1980) set all-time box office records in Hong Kong with exhilarating action and comedy, the time seemed right for Jackie to go to Hollywood and try on Bruce Lee's shoes.

To paraphrase Norma Desmond, his feet were the right size. It was the movies that were too small.

Battle Creek Brawl (1980) did nothing to attain him Lee-like status. He tried again with *Cannonball Run* (1980), *Cannonball Run II* (1983) and *The Protector* (1985). He was too new, too different . . . and maybe *too* good. He was put into the hands of directors who didn't understand him or even try. Directors who let other people choreograph his stunts and fights, as if no matter how good *he* was, Hollywood *had* to be better.

"I think my dream is over . . . I stay in L.A., I studied my English . . . I almost gave up the Asian market," said Jackie in the *Important Magazine.* "But after the movie was filmed I traveled all over America doing almost a new place and a new promotion every day . . . just keep flying. Every radio, T.V. station where I go, when I get there, all the same questions . . . 'Man, what's your name again? Are you new Bruce Lee?' It makes me very tired."

Chan went back to Hong Kong and proceeded to produce hit after hit, convinced that America was a mistress he would never have.

Now . . . she is coming to him.

"It's not easy," Chan said in *Time Out New York,* about the place that broke his heart. "I'm not saying I'm coming back—I'm just trying."

Don't be deceived. Everyone in Hollywood has known about Jackie Chan for a long time. In one way, it was good to have him, but over there in Hong Kong . . . far away . . . where they could take scenes and stunts from his wildly clever movies and use them in their own without many people noticing the lift. In another way, they hoped he'd just disappear—a daredevil in another country doing what none of their action "megastars" could.

What if Jackie *did* come to town? What then?

New Line Cinema and Miramax/Dimension—those fun-loving imps of the movie industry—decided it might be fun to find out, shake things up. Wasn't it time for the return of the prodigal son?

Seeing a groundswell of enthusiasm for Chan's work without the benefit of ever having a stateside release, both companies simultaneously scrambled to pick up rights to different Chan crowd pleasers. New Line was first up at bat. They took a then two-year-old movie, *Rumble in the Bronx,* reedited it, restructured it, rescored it, redubbed it, and brought Chan in as the home-run hitter of a media blitz that can only be called inspired.

■ Man, that had to hurt!—Jackie gets a leg up in *Twin Dragons*.

"We're in the business of Americanizing Jackie Chan as much as we can," said Mitchell Goldman, president of marketing and distribution at New Line in *New York* magazine. "Once we establish him as an action star in an American setting, it will be easier for his Asian pictures to cross over."

What they failed to realize was the secret that Hollywood was hiding: Chan didn't need to be categorized and didn't need to be "Americanized." Jackie movies are universal. People just had to see them first.

The films of Jackie Chan have been called unrelenting physical drama: cliff-hanger, kung fu and Keystone comedy all in one. Ted C. Fishman of the *the Film Center* wrote that conveying this to friends used to watching Hollywood movies is like telling a forest Pygmy about the Sistine Chapel. Get your average American moviegoers to see one Jackie film, though, and they'll probably become adoring fans.

More people have seen Jackie's movies now in America than ever before. New Line Cinema and Miramax had counted on that. Jackie was doubtful. "It is hard for Asian actors in America," he said. "People did not see *The Lover* to see John Lone. They did not see *Joy Luck Club* to see Joan Chen."

But the marketing machine was out to prove him wrong, starting at the 1996 Sundance Film Festival. Shortly before the midnight screening of *Rumble in the Bronx* at the overflowing Egyptian Theater, Sundance program director Geoffrey Gilmore excitedly introduced Chan. Jackie humbly acknowledged the applause and screams, then held out a wallet and announced that it had been left in the woman's toilet and asked if the owner was in the audience. An incredulous young woman ran to the stage to retrieve her billfold and got a kiss from Chan to boot. The crowd's love fest with the actor's rare appearance didn't end until after two A.M. Jackie Chan received what no other celebrity at the festival had ever received—a standing ovation *before* his film was shown.

From there, Jackie charmed the jaded West Coast press, as well as the hard-to-please New York journalists, letting one female reporter touch the hole in his head that he sustained in a life-threatening stunt gone wrong. He topped off this visit with an appearance on *David Letterman* and a performance that was a touch of genius. After pleading nervousness, Jackie suddenly punched Letterman's water glass, then flipped onto the desk, did some acrobatics, and proceeded to spin in circles and smash six bottles that Letterman placed in front of him, finishing with a flip into Letterman's chair. People took notice. One person watching was Jay Leno, and he had to have Chan on his show too. By the time *Rumble in the Bronx* opened on February 26, 1996, everyone had to have Jackie Chan, and he delivered with a film that made $30 million at the box office. For the first time in American cinematic history, the top two films in America were essentially Hong Kong action films—*Rumble* and legendary Hong Kong director John Woo's *Broken Arrow*.

Buzz reverberated. "Who is this new guy Chan? Where did he come from? Why haven't we seen him before? More, more, more?"

More was there, more was waiting . . . but there was some confusion as to when New Line and Miramax would release their respective films. They weren't partners, after all. But Jackie, in his characteristic problem-solving way, took care of that by convincing the two companies to coordinate their release schedules.

"Now they're friends," said Jackie.

If he was going to woo this new lover—America—it had to be done gently, and be done right. He had waited *so* long. Jackie returned with a new offering in July 1996—this time a three-year-old film, *Supercop*, released by Miramax/Dimension.

Despite the fact that Miramax released the film smack-dab in the middle of the 1996 Summer Olympics, followed by the Republican National Convention—a slow movie period—with very little promotion, *Supercop* opened at number six.

"Years ago when I walked in the door few people knew me," said Jackie to reporter Eleonore Kuhn. "I totally lost confidence, and that time was not good. But for all those years, I collect audience."

In 1980, if there had been a sign at the airport on Jackie's arrival that read "All America Loves Jackie Chan . . ." he would not have been able to understand it. He didn't know English. Perhaps now, an older man, a wiser man, a man who has had many lovers, he remembers that sign and its prophetic message. And although he smiles, it is a smile tinged with melancholy. Now, in America too, he will have to be Jackie Chan. In every corner of the world, he will have to *be* Jackie Chan.

For better or worse, he has done his job well.

"Things like this, when you want it, you can never get it," he has said. "When you don't want it, it comes back. It's always like that."

Jackie Chan—the "new" sensation, the twenty-year veteran—has crossed that invisible Hollywood Maginot Line against foreign subtitled or dubbed movies, putting a whole new spin on the phrase "made in Hong Kong."

Instead of being the next Bruce Lee for America, he is the first Jackie Chan.

■ AT A GLANCE . . .

Name: Jackie Chan
Manager: Willie Chan
Status: Actor/Director/Producer/Screenwriter/Stuntman
Birth name: Chan Kong Sang. *Sang* meaning "to be born" and *Kong* standing for "Hong Kong" ("born in Hong Kong").
Also Known As: Chen Yuen Long—first movie name. His father called him Jack Chan, which became Jacky Chan at Lo Wei Studios, and Jackie Chan at Golden Harvest. (He also, for a short period, went by the name of Paul.)
Nicknames: Shing Lung—means ("to become a dragon")
Pow Pow—nickname as baby. Means "precious"
Big Nose—nickname for himself
Adopted Prince—nickname at China Drama Academy

Double Boy—because of his huge appetite as a child

Sunkist Boy—because of his sunny disposition

Date of Birth: April 7, 1954

Birth Weight: 12 pounds!

Blood Type: AB

Eyesight: Can see what he needs to see, although it helps to close one eye

Place of Birth: Hong Kong

Best School Subject: Kung fu

Worst School Subject: Math

Good point: Loves work

Bad Point: Can't sit still and eats too fast

Family Origins: Shandong, China

Height: Five-foot-nine

Zodiac Sign: Aries

Chinese Sign: Horse—said to be cheerful, popular, witty, perceptive, talkative, independent, adventurous, vivacious, energetic, impetuous, affable and honest. Also hot-tempered, rash, headstrong, impulsive, stubborn and fickle. ("Willie laughs at me and says I'm more of an ox because I am such a workaholic," says Jackie.)

Habits: Quit smoking in the early 1990s

Hobbies: Anything that catches his fancy, from collecting porcelain teacups to becoming an expert on fine wines

First Hit: *Snake in the Eagle's Shadow* (1977)

Directorial Debut: *Dragon Lord* (1979)

Favorite movie of his own: *Miracle* (1989) for directing; *Police Story* (1985) for action

Fighting Style: Northern kung fu, southern style kung fu, Hapkido, karate and judo with a liberal dose of acrobatics

Workout Routine: "I can't go jogging in Hong Kong in daytime. I have to go at night. I wear a cap over my head, pulled down, so people won't recognize me. I go running with my bodyguards," said Chan in

■ Made in the shade(s).

his fan club newsletter. "I do light weights in the gym, and I use the mirror to practice new fighting movements."

Languages: Cantonese, English, Mandarin, some Japanese, Korean and Thai

Education: Two years of Primary One. The China Drama Academy for stage performers from age seven through seventeen. Supplemental education on movie lots and the streets of Hong Kong

First Love: Movies

Second Love: Car racing

Favorite American TV Show: *America's Funniest Home Videos*!

Most Watched Movie Musical: *The Sound of Music*

Favorite Condiment: Tabasco sauce

Made in Hong Kong

AT ANOTHER AIRPORT, IN ANOTHER TIME—one without crowds and signs and screaming fans—a little boy holds a crumpled dollar bill. His other hand tightly clutches a bag of fruit—the bag his Mom had rushed to nearby Kowloon City to buy, admonishing her little boy to save it for the coming days. The dollar, from his father, he hands to a stranger by the entrance of a magical viewing platform where he can see a plane heading to Australia—the plane that carries his parents away.

Numbly, tears began to flow. He is all alone.

He is also all of nine years old.

In this Dickensian tale that is his life, Jackie Chan's family was so poor that when he was born his father considered selling him for $20 to the doctor who delivered him. In fact, they decided to keep him until he was seven, at which time Sifu (name for "teacher") Yu Cha Yuen offered to pay Chan's parents a Scrooge-worthy sum to enroll their son in his China Drama Academy—a place whose graduates could seldom read or write, where classes, instead of producing scholars, produced miniature martial artists and acrobats—masters of Chinese mime and song. The life for these "lucky" young boys and girls was hard, yet it

was an attractive place for poor families because tuition was free. Students signed on for three, six or ten years of indentured servitude—all their earnings going to the school.

Jackie did not know these things on his first visit to Sifu Yuen's. He could not grasp the enormity of what he was about to do. After a few years as a normal child in a primary school—fighting with the neighborhood kids, spending all his money on candy, ignoring math—what he saw at Sifu Yuen's was not a school, it was a fantasyland, filled with previously off-limit "toys" and happy, laughing facades—coached in the art of drawing new victims into their draconian existence.

"I couldn't resist laying my hands on the weapons in this corner, nor could I take my eyes off the group of youngsters happily somersaulting over in the other corner," related Jackie in his fan club newsletter of the day he first went to the school with his parents. "I was so happy that when my father asked me how long a contract I wished to sign, I immediately said ten [years]. What I felt then must be what kids feel now going to Disneyland—a perfect place for a tough kid like me. And then my father left me at the school."

Life was easy for the young recruit . . . at first. Every morning he was allowed to watch as his kung fu brothers and sisters ran in circles on the roof and did handstands for half an hour. This was first priority before eating, washing or even defecating. "Sifu said that if you worked hard enough, all of the waste would dissipate anyway," said Chan.

Little Jackie mimicked what the older kids did, but only at his own pace. On the sixth day, Jackie accidentally dropped a walnut behind a refrigerator and reached back to get it. Another student reported to Sifu that Jackie was playing with electricity. "How was I supposed to know that the electric socket was behind the frig?" wrote Jackie in an article about his life that was serialized in a Hong Kong newspaper. "Sifu was mad. He reckoned it was time for my 'initiation' ceremony. Before I knew it, I got six strokes of the cane. One stroke for every day that I was there."

To his surprise, his "brothers" and "sisters" beamed as he was being caned. It was his turn. Later, Jackie found out that this was the ceremony all new students went through. Later, when a green recruit arrived, Jackie also waited for the initiation. He too smiled.

The Sifu lost no time limbering up the malleable young boy. When asked to stretch his legs to the fullest length possible, just as if doing a split on the wall, Jackie couldn't do it. Sifu ordered three brothers to help. One lifted his right leg and pressed it flat against the wall, while the other two pushed his shoulders and back full force. It hurt so much that Jackie could not control his tears. Yet he continued to learn his skills—running, basic footwork, stretching, kicking and handstands.

Apart from training, the most common occurrence at the school was punishment: punishment for sleeping, for not knowing who had committed a theft (in fact, if no one confessed, all were beaten), for being sick. Punishment was usually a beating or handstands for thirty minutes.

"None of us dared tell Sifu even if we were really sick," continued Jackie. "Because Sifu's cure would either be a prolonged handstand or additional somersaults. It was really strange. Be it a fever or a headache, after Sifu's 'cure' of a thirty-minute handstand and perhaps due to the excessive perspiration, we would feel well and all fresh again."

"In our school, handstands were for thirty minutes or more," wrote Jackie in his fan club newsletter. "When you feel that you cannot take it anymore, Sifu was there with a cane to see that you keep at it, that painful feeling of fire bursting in your eyes and saliva dripping from your nose and mouth—that is a painful feeling that I'll never forget."

Jackie recalls one incident when a student hit the edge of a table so hard he was knocked unconscious. Instead of seeking medical attention, Sifu Yuen left him there to recover, or not, in his own time. The boy did wake up . . . eventually. No wonder Jackie's contract also read that if he were to die, nobody was responsible. After all, poor children were an easily replaced commodity.

Of course, being curious children, they were not always angels. Jackie tells one story about his "sisters" taking a shower. Once, a group gathered outside the bathroom to watch the reflection in the pool of water that had gathered on the the floor, each trying to guess which "sister" was in the shower. Suddenly they heard the piercing scream of Sifu's wife! All at once, the group dispersed and ran, but of course there was no escape. Sifu's wife could easily identify the group. Result: another severe beating! "Unfortunately, I was one of those in the group!"

Two years after Jackie entered the school, his mother joined her husband at his new job as a cook at the American Embassy in Australia, leaving their young son to fend for himself (much as they had left other offspring in China when they fled that place to come to Hong Kong years before). Jackie could not go with them—he still had eight years left on his contract, visions of some sort of dreamland long revealed as smoke and mirrors.

However, just to make sure young Jackie would be well tended, his parents convinced Sifu to adopt the boy—another story related in his club publication. On the big day of the adoption, Jackie's parents came to the school to give a treat to all the teachers and students—an extra plate of meat. "For the first time I was able to sit at the same dining table with Sifu. After that day, being the 'adopted prince,' I had the privilege of sharing Sifu's dining table every day. Sifu's table usually had more food than the rest, but neither me nor the other students at the table dared to rush for any of the mouth-watering food."

Sifu's adoption gift to Jackie was a small gold chain, which he took out of a box with great ceremony and hung around the boy's neck. For days, Jackie proudly wore it dangling on his chest as he trained. After a few days, Sifu took the necklace away for "safekeeping." "Yes, he kept it safe for me for many years," Chan says sarcastically.

Being the adopted son had its drawbacks. When another student was punished for a crime, Jackie was also caned so as not to show favoritism. One day, a group of the boys decided to steal some cigarettes from Sifu's wife. They all voted Jackie as the thief. "Their reasoning was simple. Since I would be punished anyway, it was only logical for me to be the actual thief. I saw no loopholes in their logic," Chan continued.

Jackie stole a whole pack, and the boys had a grand old time puffing away. It wasn't until three A.M. that Sifu discovered the crime and stormed into the dorm, searching for evidence. Of course, the evidence was up in smoke. Evidence didn't matter; all the boys were to be punished. Starting in order of rank, Sifu asked each boy who was the culprit. Each denied knowledge and received a stroke of the cane . . . until boy number three.

"He kept withdrawing his hand each time Sifu's cane struck down," Jackie continued. "Finally he pointed in my direction and yelled at the top of his voice: 'That's the culprit.' Slowly, Sifu walked towards me and asked, 'Which hand did you use to steal the cigarettes?' 'My left,' I answered. Then Sifu asked me to stretch out my left hand to touch the edge of the table and immediately gave me five stokes of the cane."

Jackie sums up his life at the school by saying, "It was bad." He told Hong Kong–based writer Bey Logan, "If I tell you how bad it was, maybe you won't believe me! If you were naughty, if you didn't train hard enough, you were beaten and starved. At night we all slept under one blanket. That blanket! Man had slept on it! Dog had slept on it!"

The little boy who would become one of the greatest stars in Hong Kong also slept on that well-used mat, along with two other future stars—Samo Hung and Yuen Biao (see sidebars "Chan and Abel" and "Bringing Back Biao"). Their story is now so much a part of Hong Kong film industry lore that their unorthodox childhood was

■ Jackie (l) and his "brother" Samo Hung (r) in *Heart of Dragon.*

made into a movie, *Painted Faces* (1988), directed by Alex Law and starring Samo Hung as the teacher who tortured them.

Chan has also said the film was *too* pretty. Not like the reality. "We started training at five in the morning and went until midnight, almost nonstop. Saturday we hoped there would be a horse race, because the teacher would go. But if he lost, then he would hit us." Jackie jokes, in a way that indicates he knows it's not funny. The common mantra at the school was, "The cane may miss your head but it's sure to strike you somewhere that hurts just as much."

Perhaps the only outlet that Jackie found at the China Drama Academy was his fleeting hours on stage performing traditional Chinese operas with his school "brothers" in the group for gifted students called the "Seven Little Fortunes" (literally translated as the "Seven Cute Kids"). Jackie was not good enough to perform on stage at first and worked in the wings. He learned his lessons well, however, and was soon part of the troupe. Such an honor meant that after working all day, the boys would be fed a hasty dinner and then sent to the Lai Yuen Amusement Park (now defunct) for an evening performance.

Sometimes Sifu would stay for the whole performance and ride back with the children, slapping each of their heads to make sure they didn't fall asleep. "His reasoning was that if we were drowsy and there was an accident, then we might be disfigured," says Jackie. Sometimes, Sifu went home early. Left to their own devices, mischief was afoot. A fist instructor at the school had a son named Tsui Luk, who was a bus driver. The boys knew that if they gave the name and number of the son, any bus driver would let them ride for free as a family member. They committed the name to memory.

Now, each of the Seven Little Fortunes would receive ten cents for the bus ride home. On one particular night when Sifu was not in attendance, the hawker food stalls (much like the hot dog vendors of New York City) beckoned to the boys after a performance, and before they knew it, their bus ride home had turned into food in their stomachs.

"All seven of us little bald-headed boys boarded the double decker bus," related Jackie in his quarterly newsletter. When asked for the fare, the first boy at once said, "Tsui Luk number 1033." Sure enough, the vendor nodded his head and went down the row. "But when the third, forth and fifth guy called up the same name and number, the vendor became suspicious. How could Tsui Luk have seven or eight kids, all bald-headed, in his family? He insisted on payment. When we refused, he began to scold us at the top of his voice. He kept on yelling and we kept on refusing. After all, scolding wasn't like caning, it didn't hurt." But when the vendor threatened to take them to the police station, a Keystone Kops scene ensued as the bus ceased to make its normal stops and began speeding to the station.

"The elder of our brothers [only age twelve or fourteen] tried to persuade the vendor to let us go but to no avail," he continued. "In fact, he stretched out his hand to push us away. This was our opportunity. We grabbed his hand and pushed him to the side and as if on cue, we all jumped off the moving bus just before we reached the police station. We walked the rest of the way home," Jackie wrote.

But the fun couldn't last forever. As the "cute kids" started to mature into lanky teenagers, the crowds that normally came to see Peking Opera were going elsewhere. Times were changing. Sifu Yuen sent his boys to the burgeoning sets of the Hong Kong film industry. There was room there for a youth who could take fall after fall and not die. Jackie, being young and short, often played corpses ("Lie down over there! Don't breathe!") and performed stunts. The boys didn't mind—working in the movies meant extra food at dinner.

"It would be unfair to say that the school did not provide food because it did. It was just unfortunate that the kids were always hungry, perhaps because of the strenuous exercise or perhaps because we were all growing boys. Food meant so much to us then. This probably explains why even today I still feel very angry and upset when I see people wasting food," Chan said in his newsletter.

With his healthy appetite spurring him on in the movie business (he earned the nickname "Double Boy" because of his double hunger, double muscle, double smile), Jackie proved to be better than most. As a child actor, he appeared in over a hundred films. When Sifu Yuen disbanded the school and followed his lover to America, a seventeen-year-old Jackie stayed with films, hoping to find his niche. It helped that he had that winning smile and a knack for getting himself noticed.

"I was always beside the action director. When I saw him washing his car, I helped him, just to let him see me," Chan told journalist David Chute. "At that time the pay was one hundred and fifty Hong Kong dollars per stunt [roughly $24 U.S.], and the action director would say, 'I'll give the stunts to you if you kick back fifty to me.' Even the directors sometimes took kickbacks. I did a lot of stunts: jumping off buildings, bouncing on trampolines. I would go and change clothes and do stunts for several characters in each movie."

Before he was nineteen, he had become an action director. "I also directed the fighters when they had to act," he continued. "Not in the dialogue scenes, only in the fight scenes." According to one writer, a producer saw Chan doing just that on a set and proclaimed, "You can act." So he did.

His first starring role was in a film called *Little Tiger from Canton* (1976), featuring the image of a scrawny-looking Jackie with a little mustache and bell-bottom jeans. It was hardly a star maker. He followed this with such films as *Hand of Death* (1976), directed by a then unknown John Woo (see sidebar "Hardworking Woo"), and extra parts in two Bruce Lee movies (*The Chinese Connection* and *Enter the Dragon*).

But with Bruce Lee's passing, action films were dying in Hong Kong, and Jackie was suddenly on his own. One night he was drinking with some friends and one of them decided to steal a motorcycle. Six people sided with the owner, who, for some reason, didn't like the idea.

"We'd been fighting for twenty minutes and were beginning to get

■ Jackie (r) gets a little spinal adjustment from Bruce Lee in *Enter the Dragon*.

tired. I told my friends, 'Let's go.' and they said 'Okay,' and when I was turning to leave, one of the guys we were fighting got up and hit me. I hit him back—*boom*—knocked him out," Jackie related in a *Yolk* magazine interview. "While we were walking up the street, I noticed my shoe was wet, and I looked down and saw that it was full of blood. The guy had stabbed me with something. After that, I changed because I decided I'm lucky. Because the guy who cut me with the knife, he could have killed me. For no reason, for a motorcycle. That's stupid. After that, I was 'Wow, I'm lucky to be alive.'"

Jackie gave up the film business and joined his family—whom he had seen only once in ten years—in Australia, filling his time with bricklaying and working as a cook. He also met his older sister, who had immigrated from China. Jackie had not even known she existed. "One day I went home and met my sister for the first time," he told one

reporter. "It was a strange experience. I just didn't feel anything for her."
Ultimately the life in Canberra was just too far a cry from the rough
existence in Hong Kong. "It was so quiet you could lay down in the
street and not get hit," Chan has been quoted as saying.

How could he stay here when there were fights to fight, buildings
to jump from and movies to make . . . in Hong Kong? At least that's the
argument his friend and future manager Willie Chan (a respected producer in Hong Kong) used to get Jackie back to the Crown colony. There
was a contract with director Lo Wei (see sidebar "Oh Why, Lo Wei")
waiting. Lo Wei was the man who claimed to have made Bruce Lee a
star.

Unfortunately, Lo didn't want Chan to be Chan, he wanted him to
be another Bruce. "No matter how high you kick or how well you
punch, nobody could be better than him!" said Chan to the *Chicago Sun-
Times* about the late actor. "After his death, producers were trying to
come up with the next Bruce Lee. As a result, we had Bruce Lai, Bruce
Tai, Bruce Table, Bruce Lamp, Bruce whatever! It's very difficult to survive in somebody's shadow."

Even though Jackie avoided the fate of being "Bruce Chan" or "Jackie Lee," none of the Lo movies were a success, though such films as *Half
a Loaf of Kung Fu* (1978) did show the Chan charm at work. It wasn't
until Jackie was loaned to another company, where he was given full
creative control and a supportive environment, producing a hit movie,
that his previous films were discovered. That turnaround film was
Snake in the Eagle's Shadow (1978), and it exists today as a showcase of
comic timing and endearing pathos in the vein of Chaplin or Keaton.

"Instead of kicking high like Bruce, I kick low," explained Chan to
writer Steven Drachman. "He plays the invincible hero, I'm the underdog. His movies are intense, mine are light."

From then on, there was no looking back. He left Lo Wei's company
and joined forces with Golden Harvest, creating hit after hit, pushing
himself, and reinventing the Hong Kong cinema at least three times.

When people were tiring of traditional martial arts fare, he shook things up by developing kung fu comedy. When the comedy alone was wearing thin, he introduced death-defying stunts. When costumed movies were stale, he explored fresh time periods of Hong Kong history with *Project A* (1984). And when copycat studios were still mutating that trend, he did them *and* Hollywood one better by creating the adrenaline-rushing *Police Story* (1985). With this groundbreaker, he took the "present day" genre away from dreadful sweaty polyester fashion efforts like *Chinatown Kid*, entrenched in the concepts of Peking Opera, and fashioned opulent movies in which people had nice things to wear and kicked butt while doing so.

"I've learned who I am," said Jackie to journalist Karl Taro Greenfeld. "And I do all my own stunts. That's important. In my movies, you see a lot of dangerous stunts, you know it's not editing. We do not use camera tricks. I want to do things some other people cannot do. I don't want to be a Superman. Anyone could be a Superman . . . with special effects. But very few people can be a Jackie Chan."

What is a Jackie Chan?

"I can act. I can fight. I can direct. I can sing. I'm everything," explained Jackie concisely to *Yolk* magazine.

Radio personality Howard Stern commented about Chan, "What's the big deal? Sure he does his own stunts, he's a *stuntman* doing his own *stunts*." True, but nobody does it like Jackie Chan. When Jackie slides down an electrified pole or roller-skates under a moving eighteen-wheeler, he is endearing and daring at the same time. How can he do that stuff and not be killed? How is it possible without computers or wires or blue screens? Yet the camera is right there proving the authenticity. For Jackie it's all in a day's work.

"You know what . . . for the normal day, I'm scared. Making a movie, I'm not scared. I can die for the movie. I don't want to die for nothing," says Jackie. "Right now when my car is under a bridge, I back up because of earthquakes—especially in Japan. Taking an airplane?

■ Someone asked for a light?—Jackie in *Armour of God*.

Doing a promotional tour is more dangerous than doing a stunt. Every day DC-10, DC-10, DC-10!"

Today, in Hong Kong, Jackie's biggest competition is himself. He is always driven to go it one better, to start one more trend, to inspire one more time. Each film is a new challenge. This drive, which is the secret to his success, is also sometimes his Achilles' heel.

In what is now a dangerous footnote in the Chan canon, Jackie almost died attempting a relatively easy stunt while filming *Armour of God* (1990) in Yugoslavia. Jackie had no worries before the stunt. In fact, compared to his increasingly bold endeavors, this one seemed simple.

"I was supposed to jump to a tree from the castle wall and swing onto another wall," explains Jackie. "The first take I do perfect. But the first take I also slide and almost fall. But because it was dangerous all the stuntmen and director say, 'Good, good, good.' I say, 'No, I want to climb like a monkey. Not slide.' They say, 'No, it's good.' I say, 'No, let's do it again.' So I do it again, jump, the tree branch crashed and I fall fifteen feet. I just keep falling and the tree limbs keep breaking."

In a chilling slow-motion account, Jackie sees the only thing that might save him. "The Yugoslavian cameraman. I know if he drops the camera and pushes me, I'm safe. But he keeps the camera and runs away. I just fall into the rocks and cracked my head."

Jackie makes it sound so simple, like "Gee, I broke a fingernail" or "Hey, I got a paper cut." It was worse than that. Pieces of Jackie's skull pushed up into his brain. Blood shot out of his ears.

"You don't know how bad hospitals were in Yugoslavia," said Chan to writer Bey Logan. "They couldn't do the operation until eight-thirty at night. So I was there the whole day, and my manager was calling, trying to hire an airplane to go back to Hong Kong, because he didn't trust Yugoslavia. But they couldn't move me because of the air pressure. When I saw all my sixteen stuntmen in front of me crying, I knew I was dying."

It wasn't Jackie's time. Chan recovered after surgery and spent a month in the hospital. Doctors said the only possible explanation for his miraculous survival was his excellent physical condition. They *did* call him a "Superman."

Today, Jackie has a coin-sized hole in his head (which he protects during fights), and an equilibrium that's never been the same. Yet, when asked how he feels about putting his life on the line for every movie, Jackie replies, "That's your feeling. I really have no idea. When every movie is finished, I want to put it out in front of an audience. What is dangerous? What is not dangerous?

"I always tell the fans and the media, 'Don't worry, I like to do it [stunts].' First I challenge myself, second thing is every movie, I really put myself into it. I have to be behind the director and beside the director. I treat my movie as my baby, it's not like some other actor who wraps a movie and then goes home, they don't care when the movie is released. No, I care. I care about everything. Until the movie comes out and I know there is a perfect good baby. Even in the editing, if I see something I don't like, I say, 'No, I don't like that, too violent! Cut it out. I don't like the dirty words, out.' Okay, when I totally satisfy myself, then I release it to the audience. Then I turn to the next movie and the next baby is born."

Jackie doesn't think he is a great actor. The character he plays on screen is largely himself. Whereas someone like Jean-Claude Van Damme or Arnold Schwarzenegger seems hard and untouchable, Jackie is charming and approachable. In a sense, seeing his films is sharing his struggle. That's one reason he ends many of his movies with out-takes of stunts gone wrong (an idea inspired by Hal Needham's use of bloopers at the end of *Cannonball Run*), as proof of just how far he is willing to go to please his audience. That, and to warn his younger fans that he is only human.

"I always show the children what happens [when a stunt goes wrong] and try to tell them not to do it," says Jackie. "I always act like a real human being. When they look at another film, even in Asia, it can be disgusting—too violent. And also sometimes they show it the wrong way—like with a gun to a guy's head and he's saying, 'Come on, shoot me, shoot me!' That's wrong. I don't think if I had a real gun to your head you'd be saying, 'Shoot me! Shoot me!' I'd shoot you right away! So this is why, in my movies, you can see people being scared. That's a real human being. I can fight some people. But *many* people—bull! I could do that, but it's the *wrong* thing. We are human and we do get hurt."

The formula works. The name Jackie Chan is now big business in many parts of the world.

You can see it *and* him on everything from public service announcements about blood donation and condom use to Bo Bo Chah (a health tea bearing his name). There are albums released every year or so (available in Chinatowns). In the United States, Topps Comics is publishing a series of Jackie Chan comic books and there is talk of toy lines.

Of course, Jackie was put right there on the Hip-Meter when he received the Lifetime Achievement Award from MTV in 1995.

Oscar-winner Quentin Tarantino, a longtime fan of Hong Kong cinema, presented the award, saying, "He is one of the best filmmakers the world has ever known, he is one of the best comedians of all time. If I could be an actor, any actor, I would be Jackie Chan."

Though obviously pleased, Chan was modest. "I'm honored but surprised because I'm still so young. I have a long way to go yet."

Indeed. But his stateside success has been long in coming.

"You know, this time I didn't want to come to America," relates Jackie. "This time, my manager says, 'No matter if you get the American market or not, it doesn't matter, come to learn.' I feel very happy now after listening to American audiences."

Jackie also listens when he is wanted for charity events. When a hospital in Vancouver needed a new children's wing, he helped raise the money. When another charity needed money, he donated all his old clothes to be auctioned. He remembers when he was young and hungry

and sometimes donations from the Red Cross were all he had to feed him in the lean times. He gives something back.

"After the accident in Yugoslavia, I remember thinking, 'It's that soon! It's that quick. If I recover I should do a lot of things.' So that's why after I recovered, I don't put off until tomorrow. I do everything right away. I started my Jackie Chan Foundation [which helps needy children] in Hong Kong. I started my Jackie Chan Foundation in Japan. Whatever I like to do, I have to do it now.

"I don't have a very good education, so I learned everything from society. I learned everything from TV and video. One day I was watching TV about an American guy, I cannot remember his name, rich man. He always planned to buy something for somebody. One day he got hurt, then he bought many bicycles for all the children. All the children came and he opens the warehouse and all the children run in and everybody has a bicycle. This stayed in my mind for more than ten years. 'One day I will do that. One day I will do that.'

"After Yugoslavia, I do it right away. I buy one thousand bicycles for kids in Korea. Next year I buy a thousand bicycles for kids in Taiwan. I like to see children happy. I will keep doing those kinds of things."

In recent years, he's devoted time to organizing the movie industry in Hong Kong against criminal mobs. Not an easy feat when you realize that the atmosphere of Hong Kong filmmaking is similar to the wild, wild West, complete with gunslingers and outlaws who would just as soon gun you down as negotiate, not unlike the world of the "gangsta rappers" in America. Stories abound of managers threatened with mutilation, producers dispatched in elevators, actresses raped and families threatened if certain personalities didn't appear in certain films. "Many of my friends in the business have been threatened by telephone and held at gunpoint," Chan told the *Japan Times* in 1992. "Their cars get broken into, they get followed by strange people in the streets. They feel very frightened." Throughout all of this, Jackie has acted as a beacon in the movie industry, setting up a stuntmans guild and serving as president of the directors guild and the actors guild and leading a march of 300 actors, directors, cameramen, screenwriters and production staff in a protest against the triads (organized crime). In retrospect, perhaps not only surviving but thriving in this chaotic, dangerous environment has been Jackie Chan's greatest stunt of all.

Jackie recently joked that American stuntmen call him crazy for doing what he does. "They always say to me, 'You need a stunt double. Don't you have a union in Hong Kong?' I say, 'Yes, I'm the chairman of the union.'"

The world of Jackie Chan revolves around all of these things. Needless to say, he is a very busy man.

Somewhere in this whirlwind of activity, he *also* makes movies.

Still, Jackie remembers where it all began—as a young student of pain, who learned to work and endure.

"[Sifu Yuen] was a very good teacher," Jackie told *Impact* magazine. "He taught me a lot. He trained my mind as well as my body. When I see him, he is still my teacher, I am still scared. But I have paid back what I owe to him."

He has also come to terms with his parents and their desertion, admitting that at one time he was very bitter. But, when he joined them as a youth in Australia, he discovered

■ Between takes in
Police Story.

they had been saving money to buy him a house for many years. He tried to understand the reasons for his loneliness.

Now, assuredly, Chan buys the houses.

Yet, Jackie, for one, never left that little boy behind at the Hong Kong airport thirty-three years ago. That boy is *still* a part of him, just like the tough street-fighting teen, the gung-ho stuntman and the driven director are a part of him. He is a pleasing amalgam of all these things, and as such, he is one of the world's most interesting filmmakers.

*JACKIE CAN TIMELINE:

1954: Jackie Chan born in Hong Kong

1961: Jackie enters the China Drama Academy, where he'll spend the next ten years working for his keep.

1971: Jackie's first starring role in *Little Tiger from Canton*

1975: Jackie gives up movies and joins his family in Hong Kong.

1976: Future manager Willie Chan convinces Chan to return to Hong Kong from Australia and give the movies one more try.

1976: Jackie is touted as the "new Bruce Lee" in *New Fist of Fury*.

1978: *Snake in the Eagle's Shadow* is Chan's first bona fide hit.

1980: Jackie leaves Lo Wei Studios and joins up with Golden Harvest.

1980: *Battle Creek Brawl* marks Chan's first attempt at American stardom.

1982: *Dragon Lord* marks Jackie's directorial debut, with mixed results.

1984: Frustrated with *Battle Creek Brawl*, Chan makes his first groundbreaking movie, a period piece, *Project A*.

1985: *The Protector* is Chan's second failed attempt at American stardom.

1985: The failure of *The Protector* inspires Chan to make one of his best movies, *Police Story*.

1986: Chan almost dies from head injury while filming *Armour of God*.

1989: Chan reaches new heights as a director with *Miracle*.

1992: The decision is made by Golden Harvest studio that Chan should take a break from directing because of exorbitant budgets and schedules.

1994: Chan revisits a former hit with *Drunken Master II*, creating one of his most satisfying films.

1995: Chan receives Lifetime Achievement Award from MTV.

1996: Third time's the charm as Chan finally breaks into the American market with stateside releases of *Rumble in the Bronx* and *Supercop*.

1996: Chan signs with the William Morris Agency and agrees to do several projects in Hollywood.

1997: Jackie puts hands, feet and nose in cement at Grauman's Chinese Theater in Los Angeles—a lifelong dream.

1997: Chan returns to directing with *Who Am I?*

■ DID YOU KNOW . . .

Sure, everybody knows that Jackie is the top action star in the world. Everybody knows of his amazing stunts and stunning fights. But here are a few *unusual* tidbits to add to your knowledge.

1. **Vocal Discord:** Jackie Chan is not only an actor—he's a singing star in Asia, with numerous albums! Chan describes himself as a "pecu-

■ *Twinkle, Twinkle Little Stars.*

liar" singer in concert. "Either I cannot move when I sing—I forget the lyrics—or I cannot sing when I move," he wrote in his fan club newsletter.

2. **Sticky Situation:** Chan has a fear of needles, yet he donates blood. He finds it helps if you scream when the needle pricks the skin.

3. **Brain Drain:** Jackie is an advocate of organ donation. But he's not sure what he'll have left, or what his most vital organ will be. "It used to be my brain, but after the accident in Yugoslavia, I am not so sure anymore."

4. **Chan's Folly:** Jackie is a car racing enthusiast and has been known to spend close to one million Hong Kong dollars to enter his car in the Macau Grand Prix.

5. **Fashion Plate:** Jackie owns just one tuxedo (costing $4,000) that makes an appearance at any occasion requiring formal dressing, from judging a beauty pageant to meeting the Hong Kong governor. "Why waste money?" he commented in his fan publication. "Nobody would know the difference anyway. Besides, I hate formal wear! Give me a pair of jeans and a T-shirt anytime." (The tuxedo that Jackie wears in 1991's *Twin Dragons* appears to be these same celebrated threads.)

6. **Brief Note:** When filming, Jackie stays in a hotel suite. He reveals that although the hotel does his laundry, he washes his own underwear. "If the hotel cleans it two times you can buy a set. So I just spare a little time every day after work and wash it myself. In this way, not only can I save money but also I act as a good example for the staff to follow."

7. **Clean Sweep:** Jackie's neat frenzy doesn't stop with underwear. He can often be found sweeping the floor of his office, straightening chairs and wiping the copy machine. "This is *my* office," he told reporter Jamie Wolf. "These people, they just work here, they don't care about dirty."

8. **Lloyd's Leper:** Jackie Chan doesn't have insurance. He would be the first on insurance companies' blacklists. "I don't care," he said. "If I was really dying, whatever money they gave me, I wouldn't need anyway."

9. **Hard Target:** Movie critic Gene Siskel has a theory that all great stars have larger than normal heads, which makes them more noticeable on screen. Chan *does* have a large noggin.

10. **Happy Unbirthday:** Jackie doesn't celebrate his birthday—at least, he doesn't like his fans to waste money on presents (most of the booty he donates to charity). A nice card will suffice.

11. **Blush of Success:** Ever wonder how Jackie gets that "fighting" look on his face? Easy. He keeps his head between his legs until the cameras are ready to roll. When he rises he has that nice purple pressure-cooker look. Another trick is to sprinkle gold-colored dust on clothes so it shows up on film. When kicked or punched, the dust flies, adding to the emotional wallop transmitted to the audience.

12. **Hair Today:** Jackie would be extremely sad to go bald. "When I was a kid at the opera school, all of us had to have a shaved head," says Jackie in his fan publication. "I've been bald for those ten years and that's a mighty long time! That's why I treasure my hair so much."

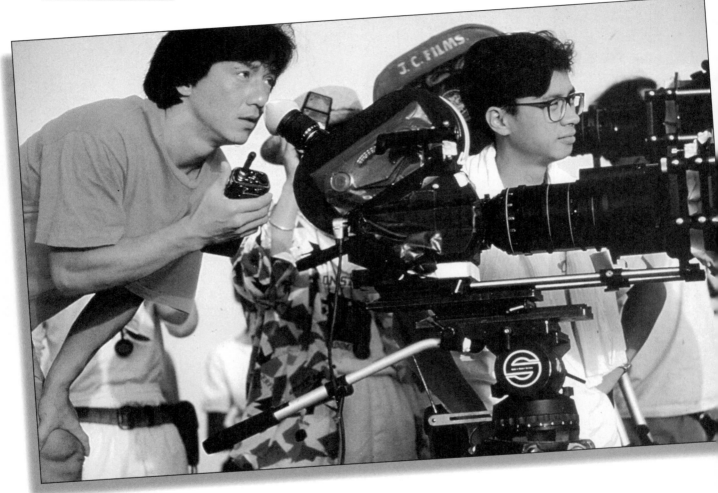

■ The production on *Armour of God II: Operation Condor* lasted nearly two years.

DIRECTOR'S DIRECTION

HE IS THE MAN WHO WILL NEVER WALK IF HE CAN RUN; never take the stairs if he can slide down an electrified pole; ride in a helicopter if he can dangle from the ladder; and always be happy . . . as long as he can direct himself.

Not since the days of silent film has there been a director who has had such complete authority, money and time to create movies in his own style as Jackie Chan.

As a filmmaker, Chan concentrates on the bare essentials. For example, when he films a chase, he films a *chase*: bodies moving with speed and grace and humor, rather than a series of overindulgent art shots. "When he shoots a fight scene, he shoots it as if it were the first fight ever recorded, without feeling the need to add gimmicks," wrote David Kehr of *Film Comment*. "Fists and feet are enough; the baroque, fetishized armament of *Robocop* would only get in the way. Though he places his cuts to accentuate movements and rhythms, the position of his camera (usually widescreen) is determined only by considerations of clarity. His technique, like that of Gene Kelly in his self-directed dance sequences, is always in the service of the moving body, which for Chan remains a spectacle forever fresh and fascinating."

Also important to the Chan movie is the Chan character. The two are inseparable. "The cop who goes all out to get his man is the same as the actor who goes all out to entertain his audience," continued Kehr. "It's Chan's eagerness to succeed and to be accepted that gets him into trouble. It is the tragedy of the overachiever, which can be transformed into comedy—into success—only by achieving even more."

It's been noted that this self-styled combination of self and sacrifice allows men to love Jackie Chan movies because he makes the superhuman seem *possible*. Women love Chan because he makes the superhuman seem *human*.

No wonder Chan's peers are not Schwarzenegger, Van Damme and Stallone, but Chaplin, Keaton, Lloyd and Fairbanks. In fact, the influence of the silent comedians cannot be overestimated in the formation of Jackie Chan as actor, director and stuntman, especially when it comes to one man—Buster Keaton.

Even though Jackie campaigns enthusiastically against bootleg copies of his movies being made these days (a huge problem in China and Chinatowns), it's ironic that the first chance he probably ever had to view the genius of Keaton was via bootleg tapes. (Keaton's work has only recently come out on video.)

At first glance the similarities between a silent comedian from the twenties and an action star from the nineties may not pop out, but upon closer inspection, the correlation is evident, if not uncanny. Both began their careers on the stage at a young age, Keaton in vaudeville as part of the Three Keatons, and Jackie with the Seven Little Fortunes. While Buster was abused by his alcoholic father, Jackie suffered at the hands of his "adopted" Sifu. When they discovered movies, albeit fifty years apart, both Keaton and Chan found a sanctuary and fell in love with the mechanics of filmmaking. They crafted their canvas to put death-defying stunts on film, risking their lives time after time for the bigger, the grander, finale.

"The audience has got to see it's me or we lose the whole effect," said

Keaton, who died in 1966 (of natural causes), to old friend Raymond Rohauer, about why he did his own stunts. "There's not gonna be any cutting away here. It's a straight-on shot. We do it for real, or we don't do it."

"All the stunts I've designed, I've done," says Jackie. "Because I know how far I can go. I'm not crazy enough to jump off a twenty-story building. Even if I can jump with four cuts, I don't like it. Jump, cut, jump, cut. I don't want to do that. I want to do it in one shot. When I'm done, I run in front of the camera—to show it's me. I'll always do that."

No surprise, both men have been described as walking filmographies, based on the abundance of their injuries. Of Keaton, Raymond Rohauer, distributor of many silent films, told writer Don McGregor, "One day I was sitting with him in his den and I asked him if he was ever hurt doing any of his stunts. He said, 'Ray, do you see this scar on the top of my head? I got that one for *The Scarecrow.* Or, do you see this one on my leg here? I got that one from *Sherlock Jr.* Look at my arm—I got that one from *Our Hospitality.*' It was fantastic. His whole body . . . "

"I have too many injuries to count," says Jackie. "I hurt my shoulder in one movie, broke my finger in another, cracked my skull in another. Even Stallone says he's worried about me. After I break my leg [*Rumble in the Bronx*] he goes, 'Why did you do that stupid thing?' But it's different. I'm totally into my job. I like movies. If I do something in a movie, the movie is always beside me. The movie is really like my lover."

Perhaps the most ironic similarity between Chan and Keaton is the fact that the movie they made that they personally loved most was the one the audiences rejected. Keaton always said that *The General* (1927) was his favorite movie. This civil war epic indulged Keaton's love of the mechanical and contained the silent era's most expensive single shot—a train crashing into a ravine. Audiences did not clamor to see it when released, but it has since been acknowledged as a classic.

■ *Project A Part II.* Yuen Wah (in glasses) and Mars (l, with miner's cap), Chan stunt regulars.

Chan always says that *Miracle* (1989) is his favorite movie. This Hong Kong period piece indulged Chan's passion for mechanics, sporting innovative montages, a single tracking shot that took seventeen hours to set up, plus Hong Kong's most expensive set—a detailed reconstruction of 1930s Hong Kong built on the old Shaw Brothers studio lot—a mountain was demolished to make room. Although *Miracle* was not lauded when it came out, it is now acknowledged by critics and fans as one of Chan's best.

Whereas Jackie can be linked to Keaton through his stunts, he is also kin to Douglas Fairbanks because of his beguiling personality and athletic agility. Just see *When the Clouds Roll By* (1919) for proof, or better yet *The Thief of Bagdad*. The influences can't be denied, and Chan doesn't try.

"A movie keeps fifty years, a hundred years. Now I can still see Buster Keaton. Every time you see Keaton, it's 'How can he do that?' Every time you see Gene Kelly dancing—'How can he do that?' I believe a hundred years later people still won't know how they did it," surmised Chan to one reporter. "That's why I do my own stunts."

This perfectionism also makes it hard for *any* director to meet Jackie's expectations. In fact, Jackie has developed somewhat of a reputation for having other directors for breakfast—chewing them up and spitting them out like they've left a bad taste in his mouth. And they probably have.

Blame his independence.

Chan teethed on Lo Wei, who was always more interested in reading his racing forms than he was in directing. Much of the choreography and pace of Jackie's first films were Chan's own responsibility. He was always a quick study.

"When I'm directing fight scenes," Chan told writer Barrie Pattison, "Lo Wei was always asleep, so mostly I'm directing everything. I watch a lot of films so I can learn to direct. I never went to school for this, I just learned it on my own."

This inquisitive mind is what eventually got Chan in trouble. When he moved to Golden Harvest and had more control, more money and more ideas, his projects started taking on mammoth proportions and production schedules—a situation that led Jackie to making movies without scripts.

"Many years ago in Hong Kong we used to have a written script. We'd all have a copy, discuss it, and spend day and night working on it," said Jackie in his newsletter. "Suddenly, someone else made the film I was working on! When I make a movie, it takes a year or more. So some other filmmaker can steal my ideas or even the script and use it. They can make a film in two or three months, and they release while I'm still shooting. Maybe my stuntman [Jackie fights only his own specially trained stuntmen] tells me on the set 'Oh, Jackie, I've seen this scene already in such and such film' and I get furious. These days I have a script, but it's mental."

Even Jackie's long productions might have gone unnoticed if the movies recouped and made a profit. When the films didn't perform well enough, Golden Harvest put their collective foot down—Jackie would no longer be directing his own films. The spin was that there were so many movies Chan wanted to make, he could not possibly do it without help from other—read that *faster*—directors.

"I've tried many times to learn American production, that is, being on schedule," said Chan to his fan club. "It's very difficult for us. For dialogue scenes, okay, but I spend most of my shooting time on action scenes. Each day we feel differently. If I'm tired, I fool around, but maybe tomorrow I'll feel good, full of energy and ideas, and fight well. That's why I can say the action scenes in Hong Kong are the best."

Could this fiercely independent Chan take input from another fiercely independent director? He had hated the experience of working with American directors who didn't know how to harness his unique abilities and tried to make him something he wasn't. He had already taken over the reigns from the original director on *Armour of God* following his accident and long recovery.

Some have argued that Chan's best films have been follow-ups to productions that he found extremely frustrating. For example, the spectacular *Project A* was a period piece to do *Battle Creek Brawl* one better, and *Police Story* served to show the director of *The Protector* how it should be done. In the 1990s a scenario began to develop in which Jackie would hire a new director hoping to be presented in a different light, only to become disenchanted with the production and then taking over the reigns, usually with a great movie . . . and some ruined friendships . . . resulting.

It's hard for him to share the sandbox.

The first sandbox casualty came with *Crime Story* (1993), when Jackie didn't see eye to eye with director Kirk Wong. He took over the production. "After maybe half the movie I found out he [Wong] was not totally in control. In the version I cut of *Crime Story*, you see the scene where the characters make love in the elevator. In the original version, Kent Cheng carries the girl to the car park, makes love to her on top of the Mercedes Benz and then some people come to take the car and there's a lot of chasing around and yelling. I told him, 'No you're wrong, that's not Jackie Chan's style.' So after that I did my own cut."

Drunken Master II (1994) followed with a much-reported falling out with veteran director and actor Liu Chia Liang, who had been Chan's forerunner in kung fu comedy. Liu immediately hired Hong Kong heartthrob Andy Lau after their parting, and cobbled together an inferior *Drunken Master III* in an attempt to beat Jackie to the box office. He did, but it didn't matter. *DM II* emerged as a lush, opulent, witty ride with traits of both its fathers so apparent that none need ask for a DNA test.

"You know the Chinese saying 'You can't have two tigers on one mountain'? That was the problem," said Jackie to *Impact* magazine. "Sifu Liu has his way. I have my way. I have my own idea of what the audience wants to see. Actually, he directed eighty percent of the movie. I took over the ending, which is very important. I still have a lot of respect for Liu Chia Liang. The press always blows things up. It's just that our styles were so different."

Yet the different style is what Jackie wanted when he sought out these directors. In the latter part of his career, he seems to be fighting boredom, as he struggles with the feeling that he's already done everything. The pressure is always there to do something new.

"Some other directors, when I hire them, a couple of weeks, a couple of months later, I know it's wrong. I cannot say 'fire,' I just take over. Many, I took over. My movie is my movie," explained Jackie to

■ *Police Story II.* Jackie patches himself up.

reporter Paul Sherman. "Every time I tell them, 'This is a Jackie Chan movie. If something goes wrong, first they blame me.'

"I hate to say 'I take over.' No, really. I feel really bad. Sometimes I really don't want to do it," continued Chan. "But I'd rather continue, to finish the movie. Firing a director helps me finish. But I know we're not friends anymore. Some people ask me, 'Why did you hire him?' But I don't know *before*. Before, when we're talking: 'We'll do a movie!' 'Yes, yes!' But when the movie comes up: 'Oh, my God. What's happening?'"

"I keep looking for good directors to help me to finish all my dreams before I'm forty-five," said Chan in *Video Eyeball*. "It's very difficult."

Chan finally found a reliable mainstay in director and former stuntman Stanley Tong. Probably one of the reasons these two work so well together is that they have the ability to bounce ideas off of each other. "He helps me," says Jackie. "If he has an idea, when he tells me, I say, 'Right, good.' If I don't like it, I'll tell him I don't like it. Because it will have to go my way. We really work very hard together. We're like brothers."

Tong agreed in a *Hong Kong Film Connection* interview. "Jackie tells me that he will give me a lot of ideas, but if I didn't think it was right, don't use it. He says, 'If I wanted someone to just listen to me, then I don't need you here.' So to impress Jackie I will demonstrate the stunts I want him to do. If I get hurt, I earn his respect."

Jackie warmed to his role of being the force behind the director. As he related to reporter Paul Sherman, "When I was directing, you know what I was doing? I spent six months on casting, location, everything!! Then on the set, it was: 'Director, Maggie wants to pee.' 'Ah, go pee.' 'Director, she wants to go home, what time can you release her?' 'Two o'clock.' I hated doing these kinds of things," Jackie told *Video Eyeball*. "Now, when I'm on the set, I just sit down. Somebody asks me, I say 'See the director.' I'm quite happy. I'm quicker making films."

Chan's self-directed masterpieces changed the course of Hong Kong cinema, and indeed world cinema. When things need to be shaken up again, maybe Jackie won't be able to avoid the tantalizing temptation of taking up those director's reins.

"Yeah, direct. I believe I'm a very good director, and also a fight choreographer," Jackie said in *Video Eyeball*. "I'm not the best; at least I know what I'm doing."

■ Jackie gives a little demonstration in *Police Story III: Supercop*.

TWIST OF SUCCESS

LISTENING TO JACKIE CHAN TALK ABOUT HIS VARIOUS INJURIES, you might think you've been magically transported to the local emergency room. "After I do a fall, one finger goes *this* way, one finger goes *this* way, one finger goes *that* way," he told *The Chicago Tribune*. "I can't say 'cut' because then we have to do it again."

Yes, he has had his share of breaks "from the top of my head to the bottom of my feet," leaving a lasting impression to say the least—not only on film, but on Jackie's body as well. Here's a sampling.

Hair
Singed and burned. *Drunken Master II.*

Head
Fractured skull. *Armour of God.* Cuts from crashing through billboard. *Police Story II.*

Eyebrows
Burned off by exploding cars. *Thunderbolt.*

Right Eye
Scratched by bamboo. *Miracle.*

Left Eye
Cut. *Drunken Master.*

Right ear
Partial hearing loss. *Armour of God.*

Nose

Broken three times. *Dragon Fist.* "Do you think I was born with this nose?" jokes Chan.

Cheeks

Cuts and scars from broken bottles. *Rumble in the Bronx.*

Jaw

Dislocated.

Upper Lip

Cut by off-course ladder. *First Strike.*

Teeth

Cap knocked out. *Snake in the Eagle's Shadow.*

Neck

Sprained. *Rumble in the Bronx.*

Collarbone

Fractured. *Supercop.*

Right shoulder

Pulled. *Thunderbolt.*

Back

Sprained. *Police Story.*

Elbows

Both broken. "The bone came out," Jackie has said nonchalantly.

Right Hand

Slashed by snowboard. *First Strike.*

Right and Left Hands

Badly burned. *Police Story.*

Fingers

Five broken. *Project A.*

Chest

Miscellaneous cracked ribs. Bleeding chest from repeated blows. *Operation Condor.*

Back

Twisted. *Thunderbolt. Police Story.*

Hip

Dislocated. *Magnificent Bodyguards.*

Leg

Wire through leg. *Armour of God II: Operation Condor.*

Left Foot

Broken. *City Hunter.*

Right Ankle

Broken. *Rumble in the Bronx.*

Toes

Broken too many times to keep count.

Chan takes a licking and keeps on kicking—despite enduring pain from injuries not given proper time to heal. But at what cost? Most mornings he manages to stand upright only after doing chin-ups on an overhead bar. His bathroom also has a stretching rail where he slowly and painfully snaps and pops his injured body into a somewhat erect posture. Sometimes his body won't snap up and he brushes his teeth bent over, parallel to the basin.

"What a true description," manager Willie Chan told one reporter. "I've taken Jackie to many doctors myself, but they all say that such old injuries need time to heal, but alas . . . time for medical treatment is something that Jackie just can't afford at the present."

Kids, don't try those stunts at home.

■ Jackie's explosive body of evidence in *Armour of God*

Comics Preview

THE SPECIAL EFFECTS TRICKERY IN *Forrest Gump* so depressed Jackie Chan that he felt like quitting. "We are very poor, what can I do?" he told journalist John Leicester. "The only choice I have is dangerous stunts."

Well, yes *and* no.

How about a cartoon, or better yet, a comic book character based on the man? After all, 'toons are practically indestructible, if you want to believe *Roger the Rabbit* and *Space Jam*! So here's the two-dimensional Jackie as an adventurer à la Indiana Jones—the one that comes alive on the comic book page—the one that has the unlimited special effects budget in this peek at Topps Comics official comic: *Jackie Chan's: Spartan X*.

(Artwork: Michael Golden. Original concept by Jackie Chan, Ric Meyers, Renée Witterstaetter and Michael Golden.)

■ Jackie drives a point home in *Police Story*.

SOUND BITES

MOST REPORTERS LEAVING A CHAN INTERVIEW, thrilled to still be in one piece after dodging Jackie's emphatic style of imparting information, say the same thing—he's so *honest*! He is one movie star not afraid to say what's on his mind. So before he is struck with the "political correctness" bug, let's enjoy the outspoken Mr. Chan, as reported in various magazines and periodicals the world over.

On Medicine . . .

"If I have a headache, I take a pill in the stomach, how can it go in the head?"

On Injuries . . .

"Yes, I've been injured everywhere. I think in Hollywood, they still have sixty-year-old action star like Clint Eastwood. But I think for me, two or three years and I have to retire."

On Special Effects . . .

"Steven Spielberg, George Lucas, they want to make movies with

me, with the computer. I wonder, what the hell's going on, because special effects for me in my mind is a zero. I don't know how to do it. I want people to come out of the movie thinking, 'Jackie Chan is good' not 'The special effects are good.'"

On Worthy Opponents . . .

"Bill Wallace—he is a good fighter, but I don't think that our fighting styles work well together on screen. Wong Jang Lee and Whang In Shik are both very good kickers and great martial artists. Also Benny Urquidez. He's really good!" (See movie entries for opponents' backgrounds.)

On Obsessive Fans . . .

"I acknowledge their devotion. I have power over them, and I stay aware of that. I try to lead a very careful private life. I'm terrified about the suicides that have happened over me. One girl tried to kill herself at Golden Harvest, and another succeeded. As a result I'm desperate to make sure that that kind of thing never happens again. There's no telling what some of the more extreme Japanese fans might do if something really unexpected happened. I can't do anything drastic, like announcing a marriage, or do anything else that might push them into irrational actions."

On Hong Kong's Changeover in 1997 . . .

"I'm not a politician. I have alot of confidence nothing will happen in 1997 in Hong Kong. But alot of old people say there will be problems. They're still going to need people to make films then. By that time, I may only direct films. If they don't let me, I'll be swimming to Japan or America."

On Tiananmen Square . . .

"Just imagine—machine guns, tanks, endless bullets against a group of helpless and defenseless students! The Chinese Government

must have gone out of it's mind! For once, I wish I were one of the movie heroes come to life. I wish I were Superman or Batman—then perhaps I could ward off bullets. Hearts of the people are not won through bullets. It is Peace, not war, which will help to make China the great nation that it has struggled so hard to become."

On Hong Kong Triads . . .

"I told the triads, 'My address is here. Come to destroy my office.' They don't do it." (In 1992, Chan led more than three hundred people on a march against police headquarters to protest the triad corruption in the Hong Kong film industry.)

On Bruce Lee . . .

"With all due respect to Bruce, I do not like to be the 'new' Bruce Lee but I will certainly like to carry on his work. Bruce brought Chinese movies to international acclaim and I would like to continue where he left off. My hope is that years from now, when people turn the pages of the HK movie industry, somewhere below Bruce Lee's name, there is also the name of Jackie Chan."

On Kung Fu Movies . . .

"We do not term the films we make 'kung fu films' anymore. We now call them 'action films' instead."

On Action Movies . . .

"You can ask an audience, if they go see my action movies, who do they really watch? They say 'Jackie Chan.' I'm quite happy about that. You can't say that about people who watch *Star Wars* or other special effects movies. They don't remember the actors . . . they go to see a Spielberg movie. In America, they don't have action movies. They have action *special effects* movies. If you want action movies, watch Jackie Chan. Special effects—America."

■ On the edge in
Police Story.

On Favorite Action Actors . . .

"I like Bruce Lee. He did everything—wrote, acted, directed. And in America, I like Stallone. Like me, he does everything—acts, fights and good talking. But I really admire Lee."

On Arnold Schwarzenegger . . .

"Schwarzenegger doesn't know how to fight. I don't think I could defeat him. He's too big. But I can do a lot of things that he cannot do. Stunt things. Jumping. I can flip off the wall. I'm faster. I think I can punch him three times and he only has one punch."

On Fighting Mike Tyson . . .

"No, no way. If I could kick and it's outside a ring, then it's different.

The difference between boxing and kung fu is that in kung fu, we have everything—grabbing, kicking. With boxing, no legs. How can I fight with no *legs*? Tyson—he's technically very good."

On Bruce Willis . . .

"*Die Hard*—when he has to walk across the glass bare-footed, that's good, but that's a good writer and good director. That's not Bruce Willis. That Hawk [*Hudson Hawk*] movie was no good. I don't like that. Different director changes everything."

On Jean-Claude Van Damme . . .

"I think he's a good fighter, not a good stuntman. He's always the same—one emotion. And I don't think he does his own stunts."

On Steven Seagal . . .

"His fighting scenes are very good, though I hear he has become a little bit fat. I thought that last movie with him on the ship was great [*Under Siege*]."

On Sylvester Stallone . . .

"He's big. Very big. I couldn't hurt him. But I'm faster than him."

On Product Endorsement . . .

"My image is established through many years of hard work. I will not have it tarnished for a few million dollars! Perhaps, if it's a few billion, then I might consider."

On Investing . . .

"I missed the chance [to invest in real estate]. I'm not a good investor. I have a lot of rich friends who keep telling me of good investments, but I only want to make movies."

■ During a
quiet moment
on the set of
My Lucky Stars.

On Holidays . . .

"I just hate holidays . . . at this point in my life these things are not that important to me. I feel that if you are happy, everyday can be a

X-mas or a New Year. What good would it be if you are only kind to someone on his or her birthday, love him or her only on Valentine's Day or are filial to your parents only on Father's or Mother's Day? If you really care for someone, it should be an everyday thing."

On Unions . . .

"Everything is unionized in America—good for the individual but costly for the company! If only we could strike a happy medium between the two systems."

On Making Movies in America . . .

"I only saw that they spent too much money. Every day there would be helicopters flying in over the mountains from Las Vegas to bring us lunch [while filming *Cannonball Run*]. As soon as I heard the helicopters, I knew it was lunch time. Red wine. White wine. Beef. Chicken. Shrimps. Crazy to spend that much money for lunch."

On His AIDS/Condom Commercials . . .

"I want people to live a long time. Be happy. Go see my movies."

On His Private Life . . .

"I always used to say, 'No personal question!' Before, I lied. Journalist ask me, 'Do you have a girlfriend?' I say no! 'You have a wife?' No! Because the first time I admit I have a girlfriend, one of my girl fans commit suicide! Jump to the subway! Another girl drink poison in front of my office. But now? Now I will tell the truth. I have a girlfriend. And I have a wife! Very good wife! And I have a son. Twelve years old."

JACKIE CHAN FILM CHECKLIST

JACKIE CHAN STARTED HIS FILM CAREER at the age of seven as a child actor, and appeared in over a hundred films, starting with his breaks in *Big and Little Wong Tin-Bar* (1962) and a bit part in *The World of Suzie Wong* (1964), and including such forgettable movies as *The Love Eternal* (1963) as well as a few "blue" movies for Shaw Brothers Studio such as *Golden Lotus*, before moving on to Lo Wei Studios and Golden Harvest Studios.

"Our opera school was a popular place for directors and producers to come to pick a child actor if they needed one," Jackie said in a recent interview. He also has said, frankly, that he cannot tell you how many movies he did as a child or a bit player, but unfortunately, there was none that he was proud of.

Indeed, don't expect his early efforts to be slick Hollywood-style movies. They're not. Production values, even in recent Hong Kong films, have never been paramount. Often, the "heart" in these movies makes up for grainy film. Be open-minded, and look for the enjoyment inherent in discovering something new.

This checklist will hit upon all the movies that deserve mention, and go into various depth depending on how important that movie was to

Jackie's overall career. For example, movies in which he was merely a stuntman will be mentioned briefly, while movies for which he was actor, writer, director, editor and basically *god* will, of course, merit more space.

Taking into account that each individual's enjoyment of a movie is a personal experience that is hard to measure, we'll still endeavor to categorize the movies using the following fists-in-the-face criteria:

Fists in the Face:

🤛 —poor action

🤛🤛 —fair action

🤛🤛🤛 —good action

🤛🤛🤛🤛 —very good action

🤛🤛🤛🤛🤛 —excellent action

■ BIG AND LITTLE WONG TIN-BAR
(1962)

At age eight, Chan was chosen by Li Li Hwa, a Taiwanese actress, to play her son in this traditional family drama.

■ THE LOVE ETERNAL
(1963)

Bit part.

■ THE STORY OF QUI XIANGLIN
(1964)

Bit part.

■ A TOUCH OF ZEN
(1968)

Stuntman.

■ ATTACK OF THE KUNG FU GIRLS
(1971)

Bit part.

■ FISTS OF FURY
(1971; called *The Chinese Connection* in America.)

Stuntman. Jackie works with the legendary Bruce Lee.

■ That's Jackie on the far left in *Attack of the Kung Fu Girls*.

■ THE LITTLE TIGER OF GUANGDONG
(1971; aka *Little Tiger from Canton* and *Stranger in Hong Kong*)

Directed by Chin Hsin. Martial arts directors Chan Yuen Long, Se Fu Yai. Starring Chen Yuan Long, Juan Hsao Ten, Shth Tien, Han Kuo Tsi, Yuen Bill, Chang Chin, Kuen Yung Man.

The premise: A murder occurs among a trio of gangsters, leaving a young orphaned boy (Chan) to be raised by the remaining criminal after the slayer runs away. When the culprit returns, it's up to Jackie, in his first leading role, to avenge his father's death.

Best action: Straight karate kicks and punches, popularized by action films in the 1970s, abound. Absent are the fluid acrobatics of Jackie's opera school training. **Film fact:** Wasn't considered releasable until after Chan attained stardom, when it was purchased by an unscrupulous producer who edited in fresh footage to create a "new" movie released under the aka titles above. **Jackie says:** "To this point, I know fighting only. When it comes to film, I'm like a student," Chan told writer Neva Friedman. **Bottom line:** It's a young Jackie Chan with bell-bottom jeans—all that's missing is a Clearasil moment in between fights. Strictly a novelty item.

Rating: 👊

■ HAPKIDO
(1972)

Bit part.

■ NOT SCARED TO DIE
(1973; aka *Eagle's Shadow Fist*)

Directed by Zhu Wu (aka Heng Tsu). Starring Wang Qing and Chen Yeun Long.

The premise: Based on the true story of a troupe of actors performing patriotic plays during the Japanese occupation of China during World War II. We never get to see a performance, as the actors are raided and forced to hide out in a small village. All's well until two Japanese karate masters start to oppress the town.

Film fact: After the huge success of *Snake in the Eagle's Shadow* (1978), this film was rereleased as *Eagle's Shadow Fist.* **Bottom line:** Shows the *slightest* hint of the great career to come . . . but probably only in hindsight. From the very beginning, when new photos of Jackie are splashed across the opening credits of this much older film, you know you are in trouble. The sight of a nineteen-year-old Jackie is *almost* worth the price of a video rental—he steals every scene he enters—jumping like a human Ping-Pong ball, sporting hair that is still growing out from his school days. Be warned, this is a particularly bloody and needlessly brutal movie.

Rating: 👊

■ THE HEROINE
(1973)

Martial arts instructor. Second male lead.

■ ENTER THE DRAGON
(1973)

Bit part, stuntman. Jackie has the distinction of having his neck broken by Bruce Lee.

■ THE YOUNG DRAGONS
(1973)

Choreographer.

■ GOLDEN LOTUS
(1974)

Bit part.

■ THE HIMALAYAN
(1975)

Bit part, stuntman.

■ ALL IN THE FAMILY
(1975)

Supporting role. Jackie is chased by sex-starved girlfriend.

■ YOUNG TIGER/POLICE WOMAN
(1975)

Supporting role.

■ THE DRAGON TAMERS
(1975)

Choreographer.

■ HAND OF DEATH
(1976; aka Countdown in Kung Fu)

Written and directed by John Woo. Starring Tan Tao Liang, Jackie Chan, Samo Hung, Yuen Biao and Dorian Tan.

The premise: A formula actioner about Shaolin disciples who smuggle a rebel leader through enemy lines. Typical period piece of the 1970s.

Film fact: This is the only film graced by the talents of John Woo, Jackie Chan, Samo Hung and Yuen Biao. Choreography by Samo Hung. **John Woo says:** "I remember we had a good time working on that film. We were all young guys having fun. I certainly didn't imagine at the time that they would all become so famous!" Woo is quoted as saying in the book *Hong Kong Action Movies*. **Bottom line:** While Tan Tiao Liang (aka Tan Dao Liang of *Incredible Kung Fu Legs*) is the star of the film, Chan gets all of the best fight scenes, and even a spectacular death. Do we see a trend here?

Rating: 👊👊

■ NEW FIST OF FURY
(1976)

Directed by Lo Wei. Martial arts instructor Hang Ying Chieh, from Lo Wei company. Starring Jackie Chan, Nora Miao and Han Ying Chieh.

In 1976, Chan signed an eight-picture deal with Lo Wei, who had directed Bruce Lee in *The Big Boss* (aka *Fists of Fury*) and *Fists of Fury* (aka *The Chinese Connection*). The film packages were switched when the movies made their way to America, thus confusing people for years.

The premise: A sequel to Bruce Lee's *Fists of Fury*. Nora Miao, the sister of Lee's screen character, escapes from occupied China to Taiwan. While disembarking, a young thief (Chan), steals one of her bags, containing the *nunchaku*—two wooden sticks connected by a chain—of the dead Lee. Later, when a kung fu school that cooperates with the Japanese tries to force Chan to join, he pulls out the weapon, and is so unskilled he knocks himself out. Found near death in a ditch by Miao, Chan recovers and eventually learns the kung fu necessary to take on a fearsome Japanese martial artist.

Film fact: In his premiere Lo Wei film, Jackie's first job as "the new Bruce Lee" is to fight an extremely convoluted story line. Like other Lee

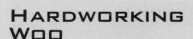

HARDWORKING WOO

John Woo, the king of "gun-fu," is one of the most famous directors to come out of Hong Kong. But ask the average film buff about *Hand of Death* (1976), and they may not even know that Woo once directed the young Jackie Chan—films like *A Better Tomorrow* (1986), *Bullet in the Head* (1990) and *Hard Boiled* (1992) have eclipsed *those* beginnings.

Actually, Woo directed two movies before *Hand of Death* and has subsequently directed over twenty, with escalating degrees of inventiveness and gunplay—the most trendsetting being *The Killer* starring Chow Yun Fat. Devotees of midnight showings know it as a lush gangster film copied in everything from *True Romance to The Crow.*

"Now everyone is using two guns. Maybe in my next movie I'll only use one gun," joked Woo in *Yolk* magazine of the homage. "But I'm glad to see my movies at work."

Currently Woo is dealing with the politics of working in a Hollywood not normally open to Asian talent. Yet he's succeeded where others have failed, directing three promising movies—*Hard Target* (1993) with Jean-Claude Van Damme, and *Broken Arrow* (1996) and *Face Off* (1997), both starring John Travolta.

Before those successes, Woo was paired consistently with Hong Kong actor Chow Yun Fat. Once this magical collaboration started, it never stopped. The two are currently planning to work together in America. Good news for action fans.

Despite the differences in creative control between Hollywood and Hong Kong, Woo says he is just happy to be doing what he loves.

"When the sun rises, I get in the car and go to work. After work, I go home and cook for the family," Woo told writer Martin Wong. "It's a very simple life. A fifty billion dollar movie or a fifty thousand dollar movie, it doesn't make a difference as long as I'm making a movie."

imitations, this film did badly at the box office. **Jackie says:** During production, since he was new, he took every suggestion from the director. If he said "Move that finger," Jackie moved the finger he wanted. **Best action:** Lackluster fights are the norm until Chan does his stuff in the last fifteen minutes of the film. The same choreographer was used as on *Fists of Fury*, thus the fighting style bears a slight resemblance to Bruce Lee with some of Jackie's athletic ability thrown in. **Bottom line:** Wei pours it on *way* too thick during the emotional scenes, especially when he flashes pictures of the late Lee in between Chan's heroic stances. There is a heavy anti–Japanese flavor found here, but no more so than a John Wayne World War II movie or even other Hong Kong movies of this period.

Rating: 👊👊

■ SHAOLIN WOODEN MEN
(1976)

Directed by Chen Chi–Hwa. Martial arts instructors Li Ming-wen and Chen Yuan Long. Starring Chen Yuan Long.

The premise: Chan is a mute student at the renowned Shaolin Temple, who needs someone—anyone—to show him kung fu. He discovers a prisoner chained in a cave who promises to teach him the best of all techniques if Jackie will bring him extra wine and food. After training with a Shaolin nun by day and the prisoner by night, Chan is finally prepared to face the Shaolin "final exam"—the Wooden Men that block the exit.

Film fact: Jackie considered this—a film in which he had some say—his first "dream" project with Lo Wei. Yuen Biao plays a Green Dragon henchman. **Jackie says:** "The earlier films were suited to those earlier times. In those earlier films, kung fu sequences used to be very long," related Chan in his fan newsletter. "I still remember the objection of the Western distributors, who felt that if a guy is a good fighter, he should be able to knock down his opponent one, two, three! Anyway, I was much younger then and I could afford to make monkey-fares [old-style martial arts movies based on legends and Peking Opera] all the time. I guess the roles I play must necessarily grow as I grow and gain more experience in life." **Best action:** Note the first occurrence of Jackie having a female instructor, who teaches him the power in gentleness. **Bottom line:** The Wooden Men featured in director Chang Cheh's

A LEE TO REMEMBER

Members of the same company, Golden Harvest, Jackie Chan was a beginning stuntman while Bruce Lee was a star. Chan appeared in two movies with Bruce Lee—in one, he has the honor of having his neck snapped. Despite *that* close contact, Chan told Karl Taro Greenfeld of *Yolk* magazine that they were not very good friends. However, one contact with Lee does stand out in Chan's mind.

"One day I was walking out of the studio and he [Lee] said, 'Hey, Jackie Chan, where are you going?' And I said, 'I'm going to a bowling alley.' So he said, 'I'll go with you.' So we go to the bowling alley, but he doesn't want to bowl. I bowl, and he just sits and watches. I don't know what he's doing. He just watches with this strange look in his eyes, like he's looking far away, like he's making some kind of plan. He's thinking of something, like what he's going to do. Six days later I hear he's died. I don't believe it. I went down to the studio, and they told me, then I believed he was dead."

Jackie says that one of Lee's main gifts in addition to being a good fighter was the gift of gab. "He could talk. Talking is a big part of fighting, of making the other person think you can beat them, of building a reputation.

I know stuntguys who are stronger than me, but they think I can beat them because I know how to talk, how to scare them with reputation. Bruce Lee was like that. You would hear, 'Bruce Lee lifted two hundred pounds.' Then two hours later, people would say Lee lifted five hundred pounds. Then a thousand pounds."

There are numerous accounts of Lee taking on rival martial artists in chance encounters on the street to defend his reputation, just as gunslingers sought out the faster draw to boost their own careers, and today's ill-advised "gansta" rappers destroy each other. The only difference is that Lee and his peers didn't use guns, they used fists and feet, and whereas some may argue that can be just as lethal if they were Lee's, Bruce knew when to stop short of killing people. One account of such an encounter surrounds Jackie's older "brother" Samo Hung. The story goes that Hung and Lee came face-to-face in a hallway at the Golden Harvest Studios. Without further ado, the two went *mano-a-mano* with such ferocity that after a few minutes Lee either showed mercy or they called it a draw, depending on which story you hear.

When asked during the course of the magazine interview, if *he* could beat Lee, Chan said, "No, at that time, I don't know. Maybe. He's dead anyway."

Shaolin Temple (aka *Death Chamber*) are more convincing as machines than these obvious men in rubber suits, flailing around like the demented robot from *Lost in Space*. Alas, it can truly be said that every penny Lo Wei spent is on the screen. However, *Shaolin Wooden Men* does showcase Chan's charisma. A campy good night's rental.

Rating: 👊👊

■ IRON FISTED MONK
(1977)

Martial arts director. Movie directed by Samo Hung.

■ KILLER METEOR
(1977)

Directed by Jimmy Wang Yu. Starring Jimmy Wang Yu, Jackie Chan and Chu Feng.

The premise: Jackie is a powerful landowner whose wife is slowly poisoning him. The only thing that saves him is an antidote that keeps the toxin at bay, and which his wife doles out sparingly. Needless to say, it's not a happy marriage and Chan hires the Killer Meteor (Wang Yu) to do away with his loving spouse.

Film fact: Based on work by Taiwanese writer Ku Lung. Jackie plays the villain, for what has been reported as the first time. In reality, he played a gang leader in one of his forgettable early movies. **Best action:** Jackie's screen time is limited—two fights with Wang Yu. The second of these is an interesting balancing act on stakes over a pit of swords. **Jackie says:** "I did not like playing the bad guy," Jackie told *Hong Kong Film Comment*. "At that time, I have no rule. For everything, I have to sit down and listen. 'Play a bad guy.' 'Yes.' I have a contract with that director. 'Good guy.' 'Yes.' 'You fight like hero.' 'Yes.' 'You fight like Bruce Lee.' 'Yes.' I want to change, but at that time, I can't.

I'm dead. I'm starving and I need to earn money." **Bottom line:** Some film historians and critics have jumped on the *Killer Meteor*–bashing bandwagon. It's really not that horrible. Jackie's been in much worse movies—for example, *Dragon Fist* (1978). On the flip side, the videotape box text on *Killer Meteor* claims it's one of Jackie's ten best movies. That's not true either. With some funny parts, a semi-clever plot, and Jackie's villainous portrayal that oddly uses his charm to add to his menace, the truth about this movie lies somewhere in the middle.

Rating: 👊👊

■ To Kill with Intrigue
(1977)

Directed by Lo Wei. Starring Jackie Chan, George Wang and Chu Feng.

The premise: The revenge-seeking Killer Bee Gang—complete with deadly darts and fetching flower masks—led by Hong Kong actress Chu Feng (Hsu Feng from King Hu's *A Touch of Zen*)—kills everyone in Chan's household, leaving him alive to deal with the bitterness of losing his loved ones. In an odd twist of fate, Chu later saves Jackie's character, falls for him, and uses "hard love" tactics to prepare him for the battle of his life.

Film fact: Based on work by Taiwanese writer Ku Lung. Became fairly popular in Japan—a J.C. stronghold even today. **Jackie says:** "Years ago, the movies were just fighting. People would say, 'Why are you looking at me?' and then fight. 'I don't like you.' Fight," Jackie said in *New York* magazine. **Best action:** Swordplay fails to heat things up, perhaps because it was filmed in the freezing conditions of Korea. According to writer and film distributor Neva Friedman, "The trampoline wires froze. Later, the picture gets a box-office reaction to match the trampoline springs." **Bottom line:** Jackie's character is somber and unlikable, but bad burn makeup and a burned esophagus do gain him some sympathy later on, poor chap. The love story is weepy and leaves you rooting for strong-willed Chu instead of Jackie's whiny girlfriend. After all, *she* is the one who agrees to wed another as soon as she hears Jackie is dead, while Chu searches for the herbs that save his life. Granted, Chu's also the one who burned his face with a poker, made him eat hot coal and had him drink poison, but you can't have everything.

Rating: ✊)✊

■ SNAKE AND CRANE ARTS OF SHAOLIN (1978)

Directed by Chen Chi Hwa. Starring Jackie Chan.

The premise: Jackie is a devil-may-care traveler with a winning smile. His high cheekbones and heart-shaped mouth make you think that he must have been studying Elvis movies to get that sexy swagger down so well. Jackie happens to be in the possession of a book of secret martial arts forms from the Shaolin Temple. Of course, everyone and their Uncle Yuen wants that book, but they have to best Jackie to get it.

Film fact: Chan's second "dream" project for Lo Wei failed to make him a big star, but it did earn him some respect in the Hong Kong film industry. **The action:** With fifteen fights, this film qualifies as one big brawl with a little dialogue thrown in to string punches together. Jackie adds to his repertoire of "everyday objects as weapons" with benches, tables, signs, a can, teacups, chopsticks and something we like to call the "napkin of death." **Bottom line:** Jackie leaps and head rolls his way through this ballet of the human body.

Rating: ✊)✊)✊

■ HALF A LOAF OF KUNG FU (1978)

Directed by Chen Chi Hwa. Starring Jackie Chan.
Lo Wei had given up hope of any success with his "new Bruce

Lee." At Jackie's insistence, Lo gave him creative control over his next movie. What did he have to lose? Frustrated with previous roles, Jackie knew it was time to change. In *Half a Loaf of Kung Fu*, he plays a character who *wins* by accident, and produces some enjoyable moments. Chan's real personality starts to show through.

The premise: Chan's country bumpkin character gets mixed up with a group escorting treasure coveted by every villain for miles around. First problem: His new friends all think Jackie is the famous fighter Whip Hero. Second problem: He's not. Adding to this comedy of errors is the fact that Jackie has been taught several useless styles by a practical jokester, only Jackie thinks they are for real.

Film fact: Lo Wei considered this film a waste of money and refused to have it released. Chan's subsequent success with *Snake in the Eagle's Shadow* (1978) changed Lo's mind. In the first two months of Hong Kong release, *Half a Loaf* grossed over one million Hong Kong dollars. The movie's secret for success—Jackie's humor—is evident from the opening credits, where Jackie lampoons the opening sequences of many martial arts films, including some of his own. He makes fun of editing, sound effects, camera angles, Zatoichi the blind swordsman, Tien Pang (the Roy Rogers of swordsmanship), and the teachings of the Shaolin Temple. Irreverent! **Jackie says:** "When he [Lo Wei] directs, he wants me to be like a hero. . . . I knew at that time that was wrong. Nobody can imitate Bruce Lee. So I tell Lo Wei that I want to change, but he won't listen to me," Jackie said in *Hong Kong Film Connection*. "He just follows his style. At that time I think I was around twenty. He wants me to act forty. In the movie he wants every girl to love me. I'm not a handsome boy, I'm not James Dean. I'm just not this kind of person. It's totally wrong . . . none of them are a success." **The action:** Chan's comic touches are obviously inspired by the silent comedians. Note the dream sequence where Jackie eats spinach and gains Herculean strength while the "Popeye the Sailor Man" theme song plays, only to be replaced by the tune "Fernanados Hideaway" from the Broadway show *Pajama Game*, while Jackie dances the tango. His penchant for using everyday objects as weapons continues with eggs, chickens, a lead pipe, a straw hat and . . . spit. The most enjoyable fight occurs at the end when Jackie takes on the villains as he learns a new technique from a manual that he must jostle around while avoiding punches. **Bottom line:** There are priceless moments when Chan's character meets a vagabond who attempts to teach him nonexistent styles, and who personally uses farting as his main weapon of defense. You'll take this loaf and wish you had the other half for desert.

Rating: 👊👊👊

■ MAGNIFICENT BODYGUARD
(1978)

Directed by Lo Wei. Starring Jackie Chan.

Perhaps as punishment for making *Half a Loaf* so funny, Jackie was delegated to making another historical romance.

The premise: Jackie is one of three men hired by a wealthy girl to ensure her safety while trekking through bandit-infested mountains. The Kicker, the Knifer, and the Puncher (Chan), take the assignment, not realizing that the enclosed sedan chair does not contain the girl's sick brother as they had been told. By the end of the movie, the "bodies" the three guards are protecting are their own.

Film fact: Hong Kong's first 3-D movie. **The action:** The use of weapons, snakes and flying limbs are abundant to exploit the 3-D potential. **Jackie says:** Chan summed up the action in this sword fighting film as "tang tang, ta-tung tung." The martial arts are played for shock value and speed. **Bottom line:** It's better than a blank screen . . . surprisingly fun.

Rating: 👊👊

SAY WHAT?

Subtitles scare people. There's no two ways about it. Put a subtitled movie on screens in Middle America, and people disappear from the theaters.

Luckily that's changing as subtitled and dubbed for-eign movies make it into more art the-aters, and even mainstream cineplexes. Of course, it doesn't help that the dialogue slapped on the pictures is *soooooo* bad.

"When Cantonese is translated, the nuances of the language are lost," said Jackie in a recent interview. "You hear 'Blah, blah, blah' in Cantonese and the subtitle only says 'Go!' or someone says a lot of things and it's translated to just 'Yes.' This is the problem. Also, after the Cantonese is translated into English, it's not that funny."

Dubbing can work—take *Rumble in the Bronx* and *Supercop,* for example. Before New Line and Miramax/Dimension, respectively, released these movies, massive dubbing took place, with Jackie doing his own voice. The end results are good. The only complaint is that the voices of some of the secondary characters boarder on hokey—throwbacks to kung fu flicks from the golden age of the Shaw Brothers Studios.

Just for fun, here are a few "Say what?" gems:

■ Acting up in *Miracles.*

"Why do you need guns when you have my fists?"
—Not Scared to Die

"Young is she! I'll help her grow up and quickly too."
—New Fist of Fury

"Bring me wine and lots of it! If you do, I'll teach you kung fu. If not, I'll tear your head off."
—Shaolin Wooden Men

"Being your slave is really quite an honor. I really enjoy it."
—Killer Meteor

"You stay here or else you get a taste of my whip."
—Half a Loaf of Kung Fu

"They were pretty tough fighters, but none of them could survive my bells."
—Magnificent Bodyguard

"You think you're a real man, but you're just a dog!"
—Snake in the Eagle's Shadow

"You're ignorant—all gourmets love worms."
—Spiritual Kung Fu

"If only we had some dog meat—it would taste better."
—*Spiritual Kung Fu*

"I made a gold sign, chopped off my leg—that's the least I can do."
—*Dragon Fist*

"You want to cut off my property!"
—*Drunken Master*

"Do you think you can beat me with your Mickey Mouse kung fu?"
—*Young Master*

"This is a telescope—good for peeping."
—*Dragon Lord*

"Prostitution should be legalized. After all, you girls work hard."
—*Winners and Sinners*

"I never go anywhere in South East Asia without an Uzi."
—*The Protector*

"Tell me what I am to you, Kevin—your dog or your girlfriend!"
—*Police Story II*

"A live-in maid—now that's good for your health."
—*Island on Fire*

■ Jackie gets the point in *Winners and Sinners*.

■ SNAKE IN THE EAGLE'S SHADOW
(1978)

Directed by Yuen Woo Ping for Seasonal Films. Starring Jackie Chan, Wong Jang Lee, Yuen Siu Tin and Roy Horan.

It just wasn't working. No matter how Lo Wei tried to present Jackie, audiences weren't buying. But, as *Inside Kung Fu* columnist Ric Meyers points out, it probably never dawned on Lo that it was "the flicks, not Jackie, that stank worse than a thousand year old egg." So when producer Ng See Yuen of the Yuen moviemaking family dynasty asked to borrow Jackie for his next movie, Lo was more than happy to agree.

The premise: Jackie is an abused orphan doing the dirt jobs at a kung fu school, while serving as practice dummy for the bullying students. His life is pitiful, his only friend a cat. Jackie is distracted from his own problems when he saves an elderly gentleman from a gang of toughs. The old man turns out to be a master of Snake-fist style fighting, which is being wiped out by Eagle-claw masters from Manchuria. Chan masters the Snake-fist style, and with the help of his trusty feline, he finds a way to vary the technique and fight for the old master's life and his own. Chan's mainstay of having the hero develop a new kung fu style in the last few minutes takes off.

Film fact: Jackie's first major hit. Ng claims that distributors in Asia all begged him not to use Chan for this movie, since Jackie had never had a hit. Ng stuck to his guns. The movie made Chan a star. **Jackie says:** "At that time, for almost twenty years I'd been fighting, I thought nobody was going to the theater to see me, but suddenly it's the right timing. I kid around, totally opposite to Bruce Lee. I do comedy. So this is why this movie totally changed the action film. This one made me confident," Jackie told reporter Barrie Pattison. **Best action:** Humor is combined with action, creating some truly hilarious bits, fast-paced and exciting. Watch for the scene where Teacher Lee puts chalk on his shoes to foul Jackie's attempts at floor washing, as well as when Jackie learns a new technique by following dancelike foot patterns on the ground. Most of the fights are highly ritualized choreography, but Jackie adds realistic touches with actual sweat, blood, and body damage. **Rumor has It:** Did Wong Jang Lee kick out one of Chan's teeth in this film? No, it was only a cap. Perhaps another more substantial rumor surrounds why Lo Wei would lend his actor to a rival producer. Simple. Lo Wei wasn't known for being magnanimous. Since Jackie had been box office poison for him, what better way to sabotage Yuen? It didn't work. **Worst injury:** Roy Horan suffered a *real* dislocated shoulder, and fought all his sword forays with his right hand. **Bottom line:** *Snake in the Eagle's Shadow* (aka *Eagle's Shadow*) shines because of Chan's endearing portrayal and the touching relationship between orphan and teacher . . . not to mention the extraordinary fights. Jackie's charmingly boyish persona is priceless. More importantly, when a comedy situation is set up, the movie pays off by resolving conflicts to the satisfaction of the audience. There is growth and closure, thus making this movie not only good, but fulfilling.

Rating: 👊👊👊👊

■ SPIRITUAL KUNG FU
(1978)

Directed by Lo Wei. Starring Jackie Chan. Choreography by Jackie Chan.

The premise: A training manual for a forbidden kung fu style is stolen, and the only style that can defeat it is the Five Fists technique, the manual for which has been long lost. A lazy student, Chan, discovers the missing book in a burned-out scripture hall when a meteor—which oddly resembles a sparkler on a string—crashes into it and unleashes the spirits of the masters of the five styles that are hiding there.

Film fact: Jackie did all of his Lo Wei films (except *Fearless Hyena*)

before *Snake in the Eagle's Shadow*, but since they were released after that hit, the time line has confused many over the years. The training sequences are shot with a superimposing camera to achieve the necessary ghost effects. **Jackie says:** As both actor and choreographer, Jackie described his job as "very difficult to do." He placed carefully timed kicks and punches into the area where the spirit would be on the processed film, achieving a curious fun look in the action sequences. **Best action:** The Chan-choreographed fights are punctuated with bursts of energy that surely drove the foley artist—that poor guy in charge of special effects—mad! When the spirits get involved in the finale as invisible coaches for Jackie, it's even more fun. **Bottom line:** The transformation of Jackie's character is well done as he goes from a rambunctious youth who fishes naked and puts frogs and eels in his shorts (you'd have to see it) to a disciplined master of the five styles. The spirits of those five styles are great fun, despite their odd fashion sense of red wigs and silver hula shirts. The plot is charming and well conceived, with an interesting array of characters.

Rating: ⛊⛊⛊

■ DRAGON FIST
(1978)

Directed by Lo Wei. Starring Jackie Chan, Nora Miao and James Tien.

The premise: Cast as a student who is dishonored by the murder of his master, Chan's character, along with the wife and daughter of the dead teacher, must seek revenge. However, when they find the man they think they hate so much, he is nearly powerless, having cut off a leg in an act of contrition for his crimes. Never fear, there is plenty of suffering to come before the end credits.

Film fact: Shot in Korea back to back with *Spiritual Kung Fu* (1978), a much more inspired movie. **The action:** Even though Chan choreographed the fights, only the ones he is personally involved with generate any excitement. **Bottom line:** Unless you want to count just how many times Jackie's character is looking at the ground in despair, you probably won't like this movie. There's not much to keep your attention, except for the crutch-wielding finale.

Rating: ☐

■ DRUNKEN MASTER
(1978; aka *Drunken Monkey in a Tiger's Eye*)

Directed by Yuen Woo Ping. Starring Jackie Chan, Simon Yuen, Wang Jang Lee and Dean Shek.

Jackie joins Ng See Yuen to create another film gem. When *Drunken Master* hit Hong Kong theaters, it grossed eight million Hong Kong dollars. Kung fu comedy was *the* thing, and Jackie Chan was its champion.

The premise: Jackie, for the first time, is the legendary Wong Fei Hong (see sidebar "The Real Wong Fei Hong"). However, this is a young scamp of a Wong Fei Hong, long before he takes on the responsibilities of an honorable life. When the antics of Chan's Wong cause disgrace twice in one day, his father punishes him severely. Jackie's further martial arts training will be handled by an uncle—the title character—notorious for maiming students and turning them into cripples. Jackie runs away from his wino uncle many times, but it's only when he is humiliated by a master martial artist that he returns to begin his training in earnest, learning the Eight Drunken Fairies style. He'll need it before the movie is through, when he must come up with a last-second blending of the styles, including the humorous female fairy style, to defeat a deadly kung fu assassin.

Film fact: Simon Yuen, the director's father, became a star in his sixties, playing Jackie's elderly, crooked-toothed, wine-swilling uncle and teacher. **Ng See Yuen says:** "Wong had always been so serious," he said about his new direction for a venerated character in *Hong Kong Film*

magazine. "I wondered what he was like before he became this Chinese superhero. Maybe he was just another naughty boy!" Director Yuen says this film was a group effort between himself, Jackie and Ng See Yuen. Their main concern was to make the film exciting for an audience. **Jackie says:** Jackie summoned up the chief benefit of this movie's success in one word—"Power"—which translated into more creative control over *all* his movies. **Best action:** Chan finds comedy in opposites, pitting himself against a muscle bound bodyguard named King Kong, a bucktoothed waiter, and a bald-headed brute. Some of the obligatory training segments at the hands of his drunken uncle make you hope that Chan considers pain a *good* friend, because it has a long visit, indeed. There is just no way to fake wrist stands and upside down sit-ups—even with movie magic. *Someone* had to do it on film, and that someone is *unmistakably* Chan. Jackie also uses food and drink as themes—from an eel to a whole table of fare—devoured in an orgy of eating as tiring to watch as any fight. Implements of destruction include teacups, wine bottles, clothing and something we like to call the towel of death, closely related to the "napkin of death" from *Snake and Crane Arts* (1978). **Bottom line:** Although quaint by today's standards, Jackie mixes the grace of Gene Kelly, the antics of Charlie Chaplin, and the derring-do of Errol Flynn, showing terrific talent.

Rating: 👊👊👊👊

■ FEARLESS HYENA
(1979)

Director, screenwriter and martial arts instructor—Jackie Chan. Starring Jackie Chan, Yen Si Kuan and James Tien.

After leaving to work with Seasonal Film, Jackie had to return for one more film with Lo Wei to complete his contract.

The premise: Chan is a high-spirited youth who can't obey his grandfather's order not to fight. Our hero doesn't know it, but the reason for this prohibition is that the villainous General Yen is roaming the countryside killing all of the members of the grandfather's anti–Ching Clan. If their style of kung fu was recognized, both Chan and the grandfather would be in danger. But young Jackie is desperate to earn money, and after ruining a chance to sell secondhand coffins (as in pre-used), Chan takes a job as the resident fighter at a shady kung fu school, where he must dress as a beggar and as a woman to avoid detection. It doesn't work for long, and Jackie must fight the general, played by Yen Si Kuan, and create a new style called "emotional kung fu" so he can laugh and cry while doing so.

Film fact: Although a technically grainy film with tacky locales and poor cinematography, the humor and pathos in this movie makes it a bona fide hit. It emerges as the second-highest-grossing film in Hong Kong history. **Best action:** Chan's favorite training sequence features, without a cut, fourteen consecutive upside down sit-ups, where, in typical masochistic fashion, he repeatedly slams his back against a tree. Ouch! **Jackie says:** "With *Fearless Hyena* I almost know [what I'm doing]!" Chan told journalist Neva Friedman. **Will you like it?:** Comedy again lies in comparisons of the extreme—putting a large, fat man beside a short, skinny one, or a person with a shag carpet of hair beside a bald one. *Fearless Hyena* stands the test of time with a satisfying mixture of comedy and action.

Rating: ♛♛♛

THE REAL WONG FEI HONG

The story of Wong Fei Hong is the stuff legends are made of, and all the more fun when the legends are true.

Born in 1847 in the Guangdong province of southern China, Wong made his living performing martial arts in the streets with his father, Wong Qi Ying. In his youth, he taught martial arts at his father's school, the famous Po Chi Lum. But Wong attained his legendary respect by becoming the best lion dancer in Guangzhou. His expertise in this traditional martial arts dance utilizing large paper Chinese lions that conceal the athletic participants earned Fei Hong the nickname "King of the Lions." He was a master of diverse styles, including the Shaolin style of martial arts, the Iron Wire Fist, Five Forms Fist, Tiger Vanquishing Fist, the Shadowless kick and his favorite, the flying thallium. He died in 1924 at the age of seventy-seven with little else really being known about his life.

That didn't stop Hong Kong cinema from filling in the blanks. The man most associated as the face of Wong—Kwan Tak Hing—made over eighty films about the character starting in the 1950s, and even starred in a Wong Fei Hong television series that ran for thirteen episodes. Kwan Tak Hing died on June 27, 1996. He was ninety-one years old. He and Wong Fei Hong are synonymous in the minds of many fans of Hong Kong film, and it's difficult to determine if recent renditions of Wong are based on the real man or Kwan's enduring portrayal.

A tough act to follow, yes, but director Yuen Woo Ping wanted to put a new twist on the character with *Drunken Master* (1978), starring Jackie Chan. This was a Wong never seen before, caught in the looking glass of his rambunctious youth. Crowds loved its irreverent nature, and the movie spawned many rip-offs trying to duplicate the Chan charm.

Then along came director Tsui Hark, who is best known in the United States for *Double Team* starring Jean-Claude Van Damme. He cleverly constructed yet another new image for Wong Fei Hong with his *Once Upon a Time in China* series starring the charismatic Jet Li, who portrays Wong as a noble, shy, but unfailingly powerful character. This is the Wong that many new Hong Kong filmgoers associate with the legend, and who can blame them? Every moment Jet Li is on the screen is pure charisma. When Tsui Hark was constructing this new image for Wong Fei Hong, he questioned whether it was an exaggeration to make him a national hero. He ultimately chose to put him inside a historical context. Perhaps Wong Fei Hong had a hard time being a folk hero. He had an enormous amount of baggage and responsibilities, with his own shortcomings, as presented by Hark. When Jet Li reportedly had a falling out with Tsui Hark and took his noble face to represent another Chinese hero, Fong Si Yuk, the series fizzled. However, Jet Li and Tsui Hark apparently made up, for they are working together again for *Once Upon a Time in China VI.*

Perhaps because of the initial success of the Tsui Hark films, and because of his aversion to the wire trickery used therein, Jackie Chan decided to revisit the role that made him a star with *Drunken Master II* (1994). It was a resounding success that builds in intensity to a climax that leaves audiences breathless. Jackie Chan had just turned forty-one and never looked better, as a shirtless, water-drenched fight in a tea house will surely attest.

"*Drunken Master II*—this film will be different," said Chan in *Hong Kong Film Connection* magazine while the film was in production. "More real kung fu. Before, I told Tsui Hark, when you do Wong Fei Hong, make it real. Instead he has everything on wires. It's like a fantasy. So, when I play Wong Fei Hong in *Drunken Master II,* I make it real. We only show what I can do. What my stuntmen can do."

At this point, we can only ask, "Will the real Wong Fei Hong please do a flying thallium?"

■ THE 36 CRAZY FISTS
(1979)

Choreographer. Note that a poor-quality "documentary" exists of a chain-smoking Jackie choreographing this movie. Not worth your time if there is money involved. If you can view it for free, go for it.

■ THE ODD COUPLE
(1979; aka *Dance of Death*)

Choreographer.

OH, WHY, LO WEI

When Lo Wei followed Raymond Chow to the newly established Golden Harvest at the end of 1970, there is no way he could foresee that he would take part in launching the careers of the two most popular martial artists in the history of the genre—Bruce Lee and Jackie Chan.

Lo himself had worked as an actor during the Sino-Japanese War under the name Luo Jing. His desires turned to film when he joined the Central Motion Picture Theater Troupe in Shanghai, and moved to Hong Kong after the war, where he acted for the Yung Hwa, Hsin Hwa and MP & GI companies. In 1957 he founded his own company—Sze Wei—where he directed *The Jade Green Lake* (1958), the first Mandarin film to feature love scenes. While at Golden Harvest, he signed Bruce Lee for the movies that would make Bruce a star—*The Big Boss* (1971) and *Fists of Fury* (1972).

A widely reported dispute ended their collaboration. Keen to establish that he alone was responsible for Lee's success, Lo claimed that Lee knew martial arts before joining with him, but that Lo had to teach him to fight for film. According to Hong Kong–based writer Bey Logan, this led to a violent confrontation between Lee and

Lo Wei at the Golden Harvest Studio, which ended in Lee brandishing a knife. The police were called, and Lee signed a paper voluntarily with the understanding that the matter would end there. Linda Lee, Bruce's widow, was quick to point out to Logan that Lee hardly needed a knife to dispatch Lo Wei.

Lo left Golden Harvest in 1975, founding the Lo Wei Company, where he signed a young Jackie Chan and starred him in a handful of movies, none of which made money. Not that he didn't try. In *New Fist of Fury*, he cast Jackie as a Bruce Lee replacement. In *Shaolin Wooden Men*, Lo tried to cash in on *The Master Killer* tradition. *Snake and Crane Arts of Shaolin* aped Liu Chia Liang's *Executioners of Death*, but met its own painful demise. Even a 3-D movie, *Magnificent Bodyguards*, didn't inspire audiences. Lo Wei did indeed try everything—everything, that is, except put Chan into a good movie. It wasn't until after Jackie's success in *Snake in the Eagle's Shadow* (1978) for Ng See Yuen's Seasonal Films that his Lo Wei films began to turn a profit.

Although Lo had "molded" Jackie only insomuch that he talked him into getting eye surgery for that Western look and caps on his crooked teeth, the time working with Lo only prepared Jackie for greener pastures. The association between the two deteriorated, and after Jackie left for the competition, Golden Harvest, Wei finished off one movie— *Fearless Hyena II* (1980) with left-over footage from *Fearless Hyena* (1979) and other Chan films, cementing the bad feelings.

Word was that Lo Wei, a member of the Sun Yi On triad, felt so slighted by Chan that he had an order out that Jackie should be chopped to pieces if he came back to Hong Kong—thus, Jackie filmed in Taiwan for a few years. Finally, Hong Kong actor and member of an opposing triad Jimmy Wang Yu offered to help solve matters by talking with Lo, but only found himself cornered by unfamiliar triad henchmen brandishing watermelon knives—a favored weapon because of their razorlike slicing abilities.

Wang Yu was lucky that policemen happened to be in the area and stopped the carving demonstration. The newspapers reported only that Lo Wei and Wang Yu were called in for questioning, nothing more. Raymond Chow at Golden Harvest eventually settled the matter by buying out Chan's contract. Of course, only those involved know if this is the real story.

Despite career ups and downs, Lo Wei couldn't foresee that he would end his life in near poverty with few of his movies standing the test of time. Now the most enduring story from his directing days revolves around him listening to the horse race commentaries instead of directing. In later years, Lo Wei devoted his time to production and distribution, rarely directing. He died in Hong Kong in 1995, leaving us with one legacy—he really knew how to pick 'em. He just didn't know what to do after that.

■ FEARLESS HYENA II
(1980)

Directed by Lo Wei. Starring (sort of) Jackie Chan.

Chan was long gone from the Lo camp when this movie was stitched together.

The premise: General Yen is back from the dead (at least it's the same actor) to practice, once again, his own unique brand of intolerance by elim-

inating anyone who prefers a different kung fu style than his own. Even the Unicorn is back from *Fearless Hyena* (at least it's the same actor), but those are the only similarities you'll find between this "movie" and its predecessor.

Film fact: A Chan double was used to flesh out scenes, and the film ends with a freeze frame of the final shot from *Fearless Hyena*'s climactic battle. **Bottom line:** Will you like it? Depends. . . . Do you *like* leftovers? Okay, let's rephrase that: Do you like leftovers that have been sitting in the fridge for a month and have green mold growing on them? You get the picture, so don't get this one. **Note:** More care was taken with some dialogue in this effort (in that it's an *effort* to watch) than with editing, as Lo Wei added a few barb-filled lines pointed directly at his former star. In the obligatory teahouse scene, the owner says to Jackie, "Look at you! Small eyes, big nose and your hair is as long as a monkey!" Later the man asks, "What's your name?" "Shing Lung," replies Jackie, which is a name that Lo Wei gave Jackie, meaning "To become a Dragon." (Bruce Lee was known as the Dragon and, of course, Lo Wei hoped Jackie would be another Bruce Lee—as long as he had control over him.) With that in mind, the boss's reply is telling: "Why is *everyone* called Lung?" No hard feelings *there*.

Rating: [No fists]

■ YOUNG MASTER
(1980)

Directed by Jackie Chan. Screenplay by Lau Tin Chee, Tung Lio and Tan Kin Sang. Starring Jackie Chan, Shek Kin, Yuen Biao, Lilly Lee and Wang In Shik.

Jackie and his manager Willie Chan set up their own production company and worked out a distribution deal with Golden Harvest.

The premise: In this first shackle-free movie away from the stifling

Lo Wei company, Jackie plays a young martial arts student named Dragon. His friend Tiger, the champion leader of the lion dance for Master Kung's school, hurts his leg and Jackie must fill in for his "brother" at an upcoming competition. During the performance, Tiger is discovered deceitfully performing as the lion dance leader for a rival school, and he uses Jackie's good nature to beat him at the competition. Of course, Master Kung banishes Tiger, who leaves in disgrace, and the forgiving Jackie goes after him. He takes the school's white fan with him and runs into a sheriff tracking a murderer with just such a fan.

Film fact: Chan becomes Hong Kong's first bona fide movie star by taking home a million-dollar paycheck for this part. **Jackie says:** "I think that after *Young Master*, I still didn't realize how big the world was," Jackie told one reporter. "I was still quite young and only knew the market around Asia—Taiwan and Hong Kong mostly. Even after people told me how famous I was in Japan, I really didn't realize it. . . . We did some promotion in Japan. Then I knew—Wow! I'm famous there." **Best action:** Jackie's use of innovative slapstick comes into its own, especially the use of props—any props—as weapons and implements of escape. In one scene, Jackie confounds his adversary by juggling a white fan from hand to hand to foot to floor. "It's so much easier to choreograph now," Jackie has said. "Then, every move had to be perfect." In the spectacular end fight, Jackie covers his body with powder so that when he is kicked, punched or body slammed, the powder flies, leaving no doubt in anyone's mind that he is absorbing the blows. Just how real *is* that final scene when he appears in a body cast? His scenes with Yuen Biao as the son of the sheriff remind us why we like these movies in the first place. **Bottom line:** *Young Master* is two movies in one. The beginning is angst-filled, while the second half is overflowing with clever gags and inspired fights. Luckily, both movies work.

Rating: 👊👊👊👊

■ Jackie spars off in *The Young Master*.

■ BATTLE CREEK BRAWL
(1980; aka *The Big Brawl*)

Directed by Robert Clouse. Starring Jackie Chan, Jose Ferrer, Kristine De Bell and Mako.

With *Young Master* setting Hong Kong box office records, Golden Harvest head Raymond Chow decided it was time to fashion Chan for his first American-made movie.

The premise: Rival 1930s gangsters hold a yearly competition called the Battle Creek Brawl to find the best street fighter in Texas. Gang leader Dominici notices the hard-fighting Chan, and goes after him as a sure-fire contestant for the bout. Chan's character declines because his father forbids his fighting, but Dominici has ways to make him change his mind.

Film fact: *Battle Creek Brawl* had an American fight coordinator. It did not gain Chan Lee–like status in the United States. "I always teach people the fighting, but when I come to Hollywood, someone teaches me," Chan has said in many interviews since. "I ask, 'How long have you been in action film?' 'Oh, six years.' Six years, teaching *me* how to punch!" **Robert Clouse says:** "In many ways, Jackie was a better actor [than Bruce Lee]," Clouse told journalist Sherri Collins. "He was a very good acrobat and a good martial artist, plus, he could handle humor beautifully. His look on screen was very much a joke-a-minute existence. It was softer. It wasn't hard like Lee. Jackie didn't break through [with *Battle Creek Brawl*], but we absolutely thought he would." **Best action:** Chan's version of a venerable kung fu bit—fighting while pretending not to fight—shines in this otherwise lackluster effort. In his version, Chan triumphs over the gangsters by artfully jostling, poking and flipping them while sweeping out the alley. The humor of the piece lies in his ease and self-control. **Jackie says:** "I'm glad I did *Battle Creek Brawl*, because I learned to roller skate. Then I learned how to skateboard. Then I learned how to barefoot ski. Now I know how to snow

CHAN: SQUARED

One could successfully argue that if not for a man named Willie Chan, none of us would have heard of someone named Jackie Chan.

No, he's not Jackie's father—though he might as well be. They are not even related, as every writer loves to point out as if everyone named "Smith" is a blood brother. But Willie has been the most important man in Jackie's life for the past twenty years—his manager.

The two met when Jackie was just a young fresh kid trying to find his way at the legendary Shaw Brothers studio as an extra, fight choreographer and would-be actor. Frustrated with his lack of success, Jackie went off to join his parents, who were working at the American Embassy in Canberra, Australia, and had been since Jackie was seven. He spent his time laying bricks and working as a Chinese cook, and there he might have stayed—not even a footnote in Hong Kong movie history—if Willie Chan had not urged him to come back and give movies one more try. It probably didn't take too much urging, since Jackie, after nine months down under, missed his friends, the discos and snooker. Hong Kong was bubbling. Australia was boring.

With Willie's help, Jackie did get work in film again ("because I came cheap"). The two worked on films by day and critiqued the day's work at night at the coffee shop of the Sheraton Hotel in Kowloon. It wasn't long until they signed a contract with Lo Wei for an eight-picture deal. Chan had found his path, and Willie Chan was on that path with him.

Indeed, Willie dedicated himself to the Chan/Chan partnership, taking language classes so that he could better handle international business, taking care of matters for which the impatient Jackie wouldn't have time, and producing many Chan movies through Golden Way. He built up a stable of actors that included Maggie Cheung, Jacky Cheung, Cherri Cheung and Joey Wong, among others. It's safe to say that many of his clients looked upon him as family, perhaps even a father figure, to be showered with Garfield the Cat memorabilia—for which he has an affinity—on special occasions. Sadly, for various reasons concerning the Hong Kong film industry and triads and the problems therein, Willie reluctantly gave up all his clients except Jackie. "Perhaps Jackie is enough," he lamented.

Today he continues to produce Chan's movies and handles most of Jackie's business concerns. When Willie joked recently that Jackie should change some aspect of his personality, Jackie quipped back, "You should be glad I don't change. I haven't changed my *manager* in twenty years!"

A touching footnote to the relationship of the two Chans happened at the 1992 Golden Horse

Awards in Taiwan when Jackie finally won the award for Best Actor with *Police Story III: Supercop*. He publicly, for the first time, thanked Willie from the stage. "I look out at him in the audience," said Jackie. "And tears . . . running down his face."

sport. I know everything!" he told *Hong Kong Film Connection*. Overall, the action in *Battle Creek Brawl* is nowhere near what it should be. Jackie knows why, as he told writer Ric Meyers. "One day it all came to a head," he said. "He [the director] said, 'Jackie you walk over and pick up the stick.' I said, 'Okay, I somersault over and pick up the stick.' He said, 'No. Just walk over and pick up the stick.' I said, 'Okay. I cartwheel over and pick up the stick. I can do that. You'll see.' 'No,' he said. 'Just walk over and pick up the stick.' I yelled, 'Nobody pays money to see Jackie walk!' 'In this movie, they will,' he said. I said, 'Okay. You want to see Jackie walk? Fuck you!' Then I turned and walked to my trailer. But I had always been taught that you respect the director, so I went back to work and did what he said." **Bottom line:** The story is uneven right down to the fact that a subplot involving the kidnapping of a mail-order bride is never resolved. Many questions are left unanswered, such as: "Couldn't they find a better vehicle for Chan?"

Rating:

■ CANNONBALL RUN
(1980)

Directed by Hal Needham. Starring Burt Reynolds, Roger Moore, Dean Martin, Sammy Davis Jr., Jackie Chan and Michael Hui.

Part Two of Golden Harvest's attempt to introduce Jackie Chan to the U.S. market was an odd rehash of an earlier Shaw Brothers effort to crack the American market. Writer Bill Connol-

ly of *Martial Arts Movies Associates* wrote that Shaws backed director Paul Bartel's follow-up to his successful *Death Race 2000*, called *Cannonball*, which in turn had been a rip-off of *Gumball Rally*. The Shaw film flopped. Golden Harvest grabbed the red-hot Hal Needham and Burt Reynolds, fresh from the success of *Smokey and the Bandit*, to put together a much larger budgeted version, with more recognizable guest stars.

The premise: A bunch of wacky drivers in wacky cars get into all kinds of wacky trouble while trying to win a race that is . . . yes . . . wacky.

Film fact: *Cannonball Run* was a big hit, but Chan's part was so small that it garnered him little attention. **Jackie says:** Chan related the frustration of seeking elusive American stardom, to journalist Barrie Pattison. "At that time, we decided whether we do a TV series first or a movie. I cannot decide. Somebody says you must do the TV series first so

■ Jackie in his second stab at American audiences in *Cannonball Run*.

everybody knows you, then you do the movie. Somebody says no, if you do the TV series then you becoming a TV star. When I sit down I just hear everybody arguing about me. You do that, do that. I said no. Don't do that. I go back to Asia; there's no question, I don't *have* to do anything." **Rumor has it:** Jackie was flown cross-country to appear on the *Today* show, only to be told that his English wasn't good enough for an interview, and that he should demonstrate kung fu instead. No wonder he thought there was no place for him in America. **Bottom line:** Chan's scenes are limited. His comic camaraderie with Michael Hui (Hong Kong comedy actor) is nicely timed but equally annoying as they are cast as Japanese characters, not Chinese. Jackie spends most of the picture sitting in a car—effectively putting a metal body cast on his agile talent. *Cannonball Run* has not aged well.

    Rating: 🤛

■ DRAGON LORD
(1982)

    Director and martial arts choreographer Jackie Chan. Screenwriters Jackie Chan, Barry Wong and Tang King-Sang. Stunt coordinators: Fung Ke-An and Yuen Kuai. Starring Jackie Chan, Mars, Wang In Shik and Chan Wai Man.

    The premise: Attaching a love letter to a kite, Chan attempts to sail the message into the yard of his prospective girlfriend. The wind picks up the kite and takes it far off course. Afraid that an ugly woman in the next town might get the letter, Chan scampers after it, only to see it land on the roof of a mysterious warehouse surrounded by a high wall. Scaling the wall and traversing the roof, Chan finds himself under attack by spear-wielding criminals who are stealing national treasures from China. This is a theme that Jackie will pick up again later in his career.

    Film fact: Originally called *Young Master in Love* as a sequel to *Young Master*, *Dragon Lord* failed at the Hong Kong box office, possibly in part

■ Jackie and those kung fu legs! in *Dragon Lord*.

because audiences were not ready for Jackie's new approach to action—sporting events (inspired by his roller-skating in *Battle Creek*) instead of fights. **Jackie says:** "I still think it is a good film," Jackie told *Combat* magazine. "Now, a lot of people do different kinds of Chinese films, but at that time I was the first one to try to make a new kind of action picture. I got rid of the kung fu and tried to put in sports, but I found that the audience didn't want that." **Rumor has it:** Jackie set the record for the most takes for one scene with the "bun pyramid," still holding the Guinness record. The actual number of shots has been rumored to be anywhere from 190 to 2,900. This is the unmistakable free-for-all that opens the film when a hundred martial artists scramble over each other to climb a bamboo scaffolding, retrieve the prize bun at the apex and return it to their team's home base. With the kicking, scratching, clawing and pyramid collapsing that takes place in this one, we'd love to know the injury scorecard for this stunt, but ain't nobody talkin'. **The action:** Jackie created three new sporting events. The "pyramid" sequence described was the first, followed by "Dragon Kick" and "Body Ball," reminiscent of football and soccer. Luckily Jackie realized there needed to be some fights, so he goes up against Wang In Sik inside a barn for the big finish, and while Jackie's character is outclassed, he screeches, claws and flails his way to victory. The finest example of "street" kung fu fighting ever filmed. **Worst injury:** In the outtakes, Chan and others are shown falling to the ground headfirst from bamboo towers and balconies, using no safety equipment, wires, or harnesses. **Bottom line:** Although a little uneven, you will find plenty to enjoy.

   Rating: 🖐🖐🖐

■ FANTASY MISSION FORCE
(1982)

Directed by Chu Yen-Ping. Featuring Jackie Chan. Starring Jimmy Wang Yu.
   The premise: It is World War II—but in a fictitious world where James Bond and Snake Plisken are real, but not available for the crisis at hand. The Japanese forces have captured major generals from the American, British, French and African armies, and the Chinese Allied Command must decide who should lead a force to rescue them. The only man for the job is Satan's Lieutenant Dwan Hwin (played by Wang Yu, of *One Armed Swordsman* fame) and his wacky rescue team inspired by *The Magnificent Seven*. If this sounds . . . well . . . unusual, it is. This

CHAN'S BEST BEAT 'EM UPS

There are two types of Jackie Chan fights: those that he directs himself and those that others direct. The difference is simple. Although Jackie's self-directed fights are exciting, he seemingly doesn't want to hurt anyone. When Samo Hung or Yuen Biao direct Chan, he suddenly turns into a juggernaut that wins at all costs—a powerful fighting machine. There are good fights in both categories. Enjoy.

1. *Police Story II:* Jackie crosses a dangerous highway, only to face a bloodthirsty gang waiting in the restaurant on the other side. Jackie uses all the tables, chair, partitions and waiters' stations as weapons and venues for destruction.

2. *Police Story II:* In the playground fight scene, nearly two dozen thugs armed with metal pipes are ordered not to kill Jackie, just break every bone in his body. Jackie goes from street to park to playground to alley as he methodically takes out every assailant.

3. *Police Story:* How many ways can you trash a shopping mall? Jackie doesn't care as long as he can break things. There's a reason why the stuntmen called this one "Glass Story."

4. *Wheels on Meals:* Jackie Chan and Benny "The Jet" Urquidez face off for an unsurpassed, no-holds-barred fight. One of the most realistic fights on screen.

5. *Heart of the Dragon:* Two fights were taken out of this movie before its release because Golden Harvest wanted to focus more on the dramatic aspects of Chan's and Samo Hung's performances. 'Tis a shame, especially since the single remaining fight is one of the most powerful Chan beat 'em ups yet filmed. The two fights that were surgically

■ High adventure and high kicks in *Armour of God.*

removed can be found on some Chan compilation fight tapes. They are equally as cool as the included fight, because choreographer Yuen Biao packs Chan with power.

6. *Project A:* The fast and furious stairwell fight shows stuntmen thrown wildly, hitting unpadded ground. You

can almost hear the bones cracking. Gold dust on the bodies adds to the dramatics.

7. *Drunken Master:* The duel with Wong Jang Lee at the end matches the rubbery Chan with the formidable kicker of Hong Kong cinema. Exhilarating.

8. *Drunken Master II:* Jackie versus Ken Lo in an intense finale complete with a fire-breathing Chan. You'll particularly be impressed by Ken's standing split. Jackie also fights Ken in

■ Jackie (3rd from r) getting ready to do a little property damage in *Police Story*.

Police Story III: Supercop (1992), *Crime Story* (1993) and *Thunderbolt* (1995)!

9. *Armour of God:* Battle with the monks in their mountain lair. This is the fight in which Jackie perfects his hit-and-spin technique, the whole fight taking on a circular pattern.

10. *Dragon Lord:* Jackie's final frantic fight with Wang In Sik is the finest scene of "street" kung fu fighting ever filmed.

movie is part of what has been termed the Hellzapoppin' subgenre of Hong Kong cinema where anything goes. The cast of characters always seems to include a mustached hero, a sexy heroine, a bald comedy relief general and a drunk, all of whom fight everything from Nazis to aliens from outer space. Be warned, this subgenre, despite its tongue-in-cheek mood, also is capable of sudden and violent endings.

Film fact: This film is memorable for its reenactment of the horrifying helicopter accident from John Landis's *Twilight Zone: The Movie.* **Rumor has it:** According to writer Bey Logan in *Hong Kong Action Movies,* this film was the second done by Jackie as payback to reputed triad member, and fading actor, Jimmy Wang Yu. By helping out the producer/director, Jackie was able to proceed with his own film plans unencumbered, and with all limbs intact. **Jackie says:** "He [Wang Yu] . . . if I wanted to do something, he would say, 'No, go and do that.' It's because he couldn't do it. If I did something better than him, it would make him look bad. I don't want to say it's bad [the movie]. Somebody out there may like it," Chan told writer Bey Logan. **Best action:** Jackie's role is a cameo, but he utilizes his brief moments on screen by flinging himself over jungle huts and climbing poles, trellises and balconies. The comic wrestling bout that introduces his character and the final fight with Wang Yu are highlights. **Bottom line:** As an example of the Hellzapoppin' subgenre, it's one of the best.

Rating: 👊 as an action movie
👊👊👊👊 as lunatic theater

■ WINNERS AND SINNERS
(1983)

Directed by Samo Hung. Screenplay by Samo Hung and Wong Pin Yiu. Stunt coordinators Yuen Biao, Lam Ching Ying and Chan Wui Ngai. Featuring Jackie Chan.

Chan focused most of his attention on directing his new baby—*Project A* (1984)—consuming a year. Being over schedule pushed back the Christmas 1982 start date for his next U.S. film, *The Protector* (1985), originally to be produced by Fred Weintraub (producer of Bruce Lee's *Enter the Dragon*) had it happened when planned. Chan took small roles in other directors' films, including this modern-day comedy, to have at least some screen time during the year.

The premise: Four men are arrested by the police: Tea Pot (Samo Hung), a cat burglar; Exhaust Pipe (Richard Ng), an auto parts thief; Vaseline (Charlie Shin, aka Charlie Chin), a slick con man; and Curly (John Shum), a unionist attempting to organize street hookers. When released, the five ex-cons set up a cleaning company to go straight, but unwittingly become involved with crime boss Jack Tar and all his dirty laundry.

■ Jackie gets airborne in *Winners and Sinners*.

Film fact: A huge, oft-copied success. This marks the first time that Jackie works with his opera school "big brother," Samo Hung in a high-budget movie, beginning a fruitful collaboration. **Jackie says:** Jackie lamented his schedule in his fan club newsletter: "They [Western actors] do one role at a time and as such, they can really study the part well. On the other hand, an Asian actor has to work on several films simultaneously. For instance, I was working on *The Protector* during the day and a sequence in *Winners and Sinners* at night—both fighting scenes! Not an hour of sleep in a stretch of three days! And this situation is not just unique to me. Many other Asian actors are subject to this same pace. Under such circumstance, how can an Asian actor possibly compete with our Western counterparts?" **Best action:** Chan shines in this cameo sequence—a roller-skating chase along a superhighway, over a Volkswagen Bug and under a thundering eighteen-wheeler. **Worst injury:** A stuntman was badly hurt when kicked through a glass window. When Chan went on to finish *The Protector*, he used sugar glass for a similar scene, and Jackie subsequently incorporated this "safer" technique into *Police Story* (1985). **Bottom line:** Having the three brothers—Hung, Yuen Biao and Jackie—in the same movie is a prelude of magic to come in future collaborations. **Note:** Some versions are missing a lengthy sequence in which Richard Ng works on mentally making himself invisible so that he can watch a girl taking a bath.

Rating: 🤜🤜🤜 for comedy

■ CANNONBALL RUN II
(1983)

Directed by Hal Needham. Featuring Jackie Chan.
The premise: Not much, really.
Film fact: The *Cannonball Run* movies are the only successful American movies Jackie had appeared in at this time. **Jackie says:** "I would rather be a king in Asia. American directors do not understand

me too well. They try to make me into another person, a character that is not me at all," Jackie told one reporter. "I thought if I make *Cannonball Run II* with Burt Reynolds I'll become successful in the United States. Didn't work." **Willie Chan says:** "The part was really too small for Jackie," said Manager Willie Chan on England's *Incredibly Strange Film Show*, a Jackie Chan documentary. Fans agreed. **Rumor has it:** Jackie was a maniac when it came to driving. Even ex-stuntman and director Hal Needham exited Jackie's one-of-a-kind auto as white as a sheet after what Jackie considered a normal-velocity ride. **Bottom line:** Minus Michael Hui as his codriver, Jackie Chan has almost nothing to do in this lackluster sequel. *Not* better than a blank screen.

Rating: [No fists]

■ PROJECT A
(1984; aka *Pirate Patrol*)

Written and directed by Jackie Chan. Starring Jackie Chan, Samo Hung, Yuen Biao, Mars and Dick Wai.

The Premise: *Project A* is a rip-roaring yarn pitting a Marine Corps sergeant (Chan), a policeman (Yuen) and a crook (Hung) against the most notorious pirate of the South China Seas. Displays Chan's penchant for deliriously escalating set pieces, including a rather devilish homage to silent comedians.

Film fact: *Project A* made fourteen million Hong Kong dollars in its first week of release. **Best action:** A spectacular barroom brawl and a rowdy romp in a pirate's lair. The showstopper announces itself loudly when Jackie does his variation on Harold Lloyd's hanging-from-the-clock-face routine from *Safety Last*. Whereas Lloyd used optical effects to give the impression of dangling above city streets, Jackie does the stunt from a fearsome height. Jackie also advanced the art of screen fighting once again by showing bouts with flying stuntmen hitting the floor, banisters, or anything else that gets in their way of a crash landing. The epicenter of each punch is highlighted

Jackie in the bar fight to end all bar fights in *Project A*.

in a halo effect with dust and sand put on the fighter's shoes and hair. Take particular note of the sustained action-chase-comedy sequence that prequels this fight. **Worst injury:** The clock tower stunt went horribly wrong. Jackie's fall was supposed to be cushioned by the two canopies, but instead of tearing through the second awning, he bounced off and flipped upside down, hitting the ground and dampening the impact with his skull. The crew had pretested the stunt by tossing a sack of *topsoil* off the ledge. Jackie could not be certain that *he* would survive. "I just don't want to go down," Jackie recalled. "Scared." Production came to a halt for more than a week while Jackie stood on the ledge every day and steeled himself. He *finally* jumped. After he was treated at the hospital, Jackie came back and tried the stunt again . . . and again. All attempts are in the final film, the most lasting image being the one of Jackie staggering away in pain. **Jackie says:** "One day when I was making *Project A*, people told me, 'We just saw the new Steven Spielberg movie and it had a bicycle scene.' That scared the shit out of me! I went and saw the movie. It was *E.T.*, so I went on and did my bicycle scene and it was totally different than Spielberg. Actually, in his last Indiana Jones film, he [Spielberg] learned from me [motorcycle stunt in *Indiana Jones and the Last Crusade*]. That made me very happy," Jackie told reported Jay Lin. **Bottom line:** A revolutionary film on many levels. First, it takes place in 1903, an unexplored era of Hong Kong history. Second, this is Jackie's attempt to make his verbal skills as fluent as his physical skills. He succeeds by throwing in rapid-fire dialogue poking fun at the traditions of Peking Opera (most notably in a rifle-buying scene with Hung). Full of stunts, comedy, great set pieces, intelligible dubbing and a great score, *Project A* is a winner. The kung fu movie even for those who hate kung fu movies.

Rating: ✊ ✊ ✊ ✊ ✊

■ WHEELS ON MEALS
(1984; aka *Spartan X*)

Directed by Samo Hung. Written by Edward Tang and Johnny Lee. Production manager Jose Antonio De La Loma, Jr. Starring Jackie Chan, Samo Hung, Yuen Biao, Miss Spain—Lola Forner, Benny "The Jet" Urquidez and Keith Vitali.

The premise: A modern-day *Three Musketeers*, complete with castle storming, sword fighting, and a damsel in distress, filmed entirely in Spain. Jackie and Yuen run a successful lunch van when they befriend Gloria (Forner)—a pickpocket with a heart of gold, who is being sought by Samo, a bumbling private eye. Together

CHAN AND ABEL

He was Jackie Chan's older— and bigger—"brother" at the Peking Opera school where the two toiled from ages seven to seventeen. But that's not Samo Hung's claim to fame. When not working with his old school chum, he has produced top sellers in the Hong Kong market, including such hits as *Encounters of the Spooky Kind* and *The Dead and the Deadly*, emerging as one of the preeminent filmmakers of the region. Like Chan, many of Hung's creations spawned legions of copycats trying to recreate his style and lightning-fast choreography.

Samo is also one of the most unlikely stars you'll ever see. He is not the picture of conventional beauty, sporting several facial scars, the most obvious being a gash on his lip. He's also rather overweight. He makes fun of his girth in movies by giving his character nicknames such as Tuba, Teapot and Moby. Yet this weight masks a fast and powerful martial artist's body. His characters are the charming rogues whom everyone underestimates . . . usually to their regret.

Although he was on top for many years, Samo's career began to nose-dive when he began churning out films such as *Lucky Stars Go Places*—a sloppily executed combination of two of Hong Kong's best-loved comedy films, *Lucky Stars* and *Aces Go Places*. The audience felt deceived. His subsequent films, like *Don't Give a Damn* and *Pantyhose Killer*, further alienated his former viewers by being racist, sexist and full of gay stereotypes.

In 1994, after a divorce and giving up a gambling habit, Hung married his love of many years, a Eurasian Hong Kong actress. His friendship with Chan, which had taken its share of knocks over the years, also seemed to be on the mend. Samo reported that Jackie won him back by giving him a set of S-Yard golf clubs that are all the rage in Hong Kong and impossibly rare. It did the trick, and Hung became one of Chan's favorite directors again, working with Jackie in *Thunderbolt* (1995) and *Nice Guy* (1997).

"Samo viewed things too seriously and was therefore under a lot of pressure. But he is fine now, more light-hearted than before," said Jackie in *TV Daily*. "He will still be the best martial arts choreographer around. Samo is Number One and I am only Number Two!"

Then it seemed that whatever squabbles existed between these two "brothers" in the past had been put aside.

"We fight alot," said Samo to writer Bey Logan, "but actually we are closer than family."

A nice note on which to leave things, but unfortunately, the sibling rivalry continues, supposedly now due to an interesting move by Hung. Jackie had often talked of making a movie about a martial artist who goes to the Western frontier called *The Lion Goes West*. In 1996, it was reported that Hung was on location in Texas shooting a movie by the *same* name. That would have been super, but the star of the movie was not the man who had come up with the title and the concept, but Jackie's box office rival, Jet Li, reprising the Wong Fei Hong character that both

he and Jackie exemplified. To add insult to injury, two years before, Jackie and Li had talked of making a movie together, until Li came out with a film called *High Risk* in which he parodied many of the important people in Chan's private life to the point of being downright insulting and cruel.

Now it seems a comment Jackie made to *Martial Arts Illustrated* in the late eighties is more apt. "Very hard to explain this relationship. Of course, we [Jackie and Samo] grew up together, so we're like brothers. He's like my big brother. No matter how much success, he still looks at me as his little brother. I think maybe there is some

■ Jackie and his older "brother" Samo Hung clear up a little misunderstanding in *Project A*.

jealousy there. 'You have success. You are my little brother. Why not me?' It's like we still respect each other, we can still talk together, but we can't work together."

And so the dynamics of the Jackie Chan/Samo Hung relationship continue . . . hopefully with enjoyable output still to come from both—either together or solo.

they discover a villainous plan to keep Gloria from receiving an inheritance.

Film fact: This film was originally titled *Meals on Wheels*. However, two Golden Harvest films that began with the letter "M"—*Megaforce* (1982) and *Ménage à Trois* (1982)—had flopped, so they reversed the name. **Best action:** The hand-to-hand combat between Jackie and Benny Urquidez—an unbeaten kickboxing champion and folk hero in Japan. A must-see! And Yuen Biao, the "little brother," is no slouch against Keith Hernandez either. **Jackie says:** "When we fought in the movie, Benny wasn't used to *not* hitting! Finally I told him: 'Hit me again and you'll never work in Hong Kong films!'" Jackie is quoted as saying in the book *Hong Kong Action Movies*. **Rumor has it:** Keith Vitali told writer Bey Logan that rather than lose face in front of the crew, Jackie challenged Urquidez to fight him in a charity match in Hong Kong. "Benny said, 'Fine, but you'd better train for it or you're gonna get hurt!' I think Samo showed Jackie some tapes of Benny in the ring and that was the last we heard of it!" Regardless, Benny returned to fight Jackie yet another day in *Dragons Forever* (1987). **Bottom line:** Action-packed—a true delight. Contains the most realistic, savage kung fu fight since Bruce Lee and Chuck Norris went *mano-a-mano* in *Return of the Dragon*. **Note:** The Japanese home video version has one scene cut out of most prints, in which Samo seeks out informant "Fatty" in a restaurant in which the round-but-packed Samo is the skinniest person there.

Rating: 🥊🥊🥊🥊

■ POM POM
(1984)

Jackie Chan and Yuen Biao make a cameo appearance wearing their same costumes from *Twinkle, Twinkle, Lucky Stars*.

■ MY LUCKY STARS
(1985)

Directed by Samo Hung. Starring Jackie Chan, Hung, Yuen Biao, Charlie Chin, Eric Tsang, Sibeele Hu and Dick Wei.

While Golden Harvest began preproduction on Jackie's next international film, *The Protector* (1985), Chan took a costarring role in this new variation on the *Winners and Sinners* (1983) formula.

The premise: Muscles (Jackie) and Rickey (Yuen Biao) are Hong Kong officers undercover in Tokyo. Following a car chase through the city, the two cops battle ninjas in an amusement park in the shadow of Mount Fuji, and Rickey is captured. Needing help, Muscles radios his Hong Kong chief to enlist the aide of his five orphanage "brothers," played by Samo Hung, Charlie Chin, Richard Ng, Fung Shui Fan and Eric Tsang.

Film fact: Did great business, making ten million Hong Kong dollars in its first week. It ended up with a box office record-breaking thirty million Hong Kong dollars. **Rumor has it:** Jackie reported that a "beaming" Raymond Chow (head of Golden Harvest) hosted a gala dinner for the cast and crew, with the highlight being the "smashing" of a symbolic thirty-million-dollar ice carving by all the stars. **Jackie says:** "This is Samo's film—he got into trouble with one of his stars—and I had to help! *Urgent* help, in fact, because we had to finish it for Chinese New Year release in Hong Kong and Taiwan! Did we make it? We sure did! We rushed like mad! Samo, a guy named Eric Tsang and myself, we three all helped in the direction, directing different parts of the film nonstop day and night!" related Chan in his fan publication. "Those were exhausting days but we managed to get the first copy out two weeks before the New Year!" **Best action:** The final fight in an upside down room of a funhouse has Jackie fighting samurai-sword-swinging ghosts, followed by a snowy room filled with white-clad ninjas. **Bottom line:** The decision to make the other brothers contemptuous of Muscles (Chan) sours the buddy element. A detour for Jackie until he gets on with the business of creating one of his most memorable movies, *Police Story.* But first had to come . . .

Rating: 👊 👊 👊

■ THE PROTECTOR
(1985)

Screenwriter and director James Glickenhaus. Starring Jackie Chan and Danny Aiello. Additional footage directed by Jackie Chan.

Chan's second starring role in an American-made film.

The premise: After a New York police officer (Chan) avenges his partner's brutal murder, he's put on probationary assignment and just happens to be on guard duty when a rich socialite is kidnapped. The trail leads Jackie and partner Danny Aiello to the massage parlors of Hong Kong and to the junks of Aberdeen Harbor. It also eventually takes them to the druglord they seek.

Film fact: Even though it achieved some success in European theaters and on U.S. home video, *The Protector* is counted as Chan's only flop since he signed with Golden Harvest. **Rumor has it:** Chan complained to the *New York Daily News* that the director, James Glickenhaus, didn't understand him, telling him to be a "New York policeman, be Clint Eastwood." Jackie, remembering the comment, says, "I'm New York police? What about my English? Every day on the set I just practice, 'New Yawk, I come from New Yawk, New Yawk.'" One source remembers Chan and his close associates near tears at times during the frustratingly stilted filming. Memories of this movie still bring out strong emotions, as Jackie told journalist Diana D. Bowman about one time he lost his temper. "I told him 'FUCK YOU!' 'Jackie, you're fighting.' I said, 'Okay the fighting will be like . . .' 'You fight from here to there.' I said, 'No I cannot.' I said, 'Fuck you! Do you know how to make an action movie?' Then he said, 'No, listen to me. I'm the director, you do your own job.' I do the whole scene his way. It's not so good."

Glickenhaus says: Right from the beginning Glickenhaus said he told Jackie that this was his film, that he was going to direct the martial arts sequences and was going to do them completely different than Jackie.

Jackie says: "He told me I'm just an actor. For me, it's just say my lines and back to the motor home. After *The Protector* I decided it's back to Asia. I told Glickenhaus, 'You do *The Protector* and I'll do *Police Story* (1985), and I'll show you what the action movie is all about,'" Jackie told reporter Patrick Z. McGavin. **Best action:** When Chan squares off against Bill "Superfoot" Wallace, it fails to please. Jackie does leap from a pallet swinging precariously from a giant dockyard crane to the cabin of another crane. As one writer put it, "Had he made the slightest error of timing or judgment he would have had about two seconds to regret it before reaching the ground over a hundred feet below." **Worst injury:** Mars, longtime member of Jackie's stunt team, dislocated his shoulder jumping ship-to-ship off Aberdeen Harbor in Hong Kong. Mars stayed in the hospital for more than four weeks. Fortunately, he was covered by insurance, since *The Protector* was an American production. (Jackie and crew are considered uninsurable.) **Bottom line:** Gratuitous Nudity. More like a low-budget James Bond film with bits lifted from *Dr. No* and *Goldfinger*. Catch it on TV if you must, but don't waste your money on a rental. Note, however, that the Chinese version in which Chan reshot many fight scenes with Wallace and added a subplot with Hong Kong singer Sally Yeh is much, much better.

> **Rating:** 👊👊
> **Chan's Version:** 👊👊👊

■ HEART OF THE DRAGON
(1985; aka *First Mission*)

Directed by Samo Hung. Screenplay by Barry Wong. Starring Jackie Chan and Hung.

The premise: Chan once again is a police officer, this time torn between wanting an unencumbered life as a merchant seaman and his responsibility for a mentally retarded older brother (Hung). The plot thickens when Hung innocently becomes involved in a jewel heist, leading to a violent confrontation.

Film fact: Yuen Biao choreographed, and although it's not the most successful collaboration for the three brothers, it *was* the most daring, as both Samo and Jackie try roles that allow them to stretch. **Jackie says:** "I'm trying lots of different kinds of film, because I'm not fifteen or sixteen anymore. I can't rely on making funny faces, sticking out my tongue, crossing my eyes . . . That's young man's humor and I'm growing up," Chan told *Combat* magazine. "I should change my image as I mature." The movie did not do as well as had been expected. "One thing I learned from that was that in an action film people know what's happening without dialogue. However, *Heart of the Dragon* was a dialogue film, so, even though there were subtitles or dubbing, I don't think people in non-Chinese-speaking territories appreciated it as much as they did in Hong Kong. I want to change, but the box office tells me not to. *Heart of the Dragon* nets one million dollars at the box office and *Police Story* (1985) nets ten million dollars. Which kind of film are you going to make next time? Very simple—I go for the ten-million-dollar type." **Best action:** Two fights were cut from the international print—one in a drug rehabilitation center, the other in a restaurant parking lot. Both are great battles that were never seen by a world-wide audience. "There was a feeling that the film stood on its own merits as a dramatic piece," said Golden Harvest Vice-President David Shepperd to one reporter, "and that the extra fights would dilute that." The finale of *Heart of the Dragon* shows one powerful Chan fight, choreographed by Yuen, in which Chan faces a half dozen gunsels and a mob of pick-ax-wielding construction workers. This is often called the best-edited and -filmed kung fu battle in movie history. "A film class in camera movement and editing choreography could run a semester on this ten minute sequence alone," wrote *Inside Kung Fu* columnist Ric Meyers. **Bottomline:** Fast-paced with much crying, and some of Hung's best action directing.

Rating: 👊👊👊

■ TWINKLE, TWINKLE, LUCKY STARS
(1985)

Directed by Samo Hung. Screenplay by Barry Wong. Starring Jackie Chan, Yuen Biao, Samo Hung, Lau Tak Wah, Rosamond Kwan, Richard Norton, Yasuaki Shoji Kurato, Andy Lau and Melvin Wong.

The premise: Four of the brothers from *My Lucky Stars* (1985) are back. While on summer vacation with the brothers in Thailand, Policewoman Ba Wah must cut the holiday short when three assassins (two of whom are Richard Norton and Yasuaki Shoji Kurato) kill one of her informants.

Film fact: After this movie, Samo lost Jackie's participation in the series, and he slapped together the inferior *Lucky Stars Go Places*. **Jackie says:** Jackie wasn't happy from the beginning. He had just finished *The Protector* (1985), but was still working on *Police Story* (1985). "Now this," he said in his fan newsletter. "Samo decided to start on a new film—him directing and me starring! So, once again, I am back to square one—with two films on my hands!"

Rumor has it: Gratis celebrity appearances by Hong Kong movie stars abound. Kao Fei, Michelle Kahn (*Yes, Madam*), and Hui Ying Hung (*Rosa*) all have roles to play, while David Chiang (*Where's Officer Tuba?*), Liang Chia-jen (*The Victim*), and Philip Chan (*Winners and Sinners* and *Pom Pom*) just pop in briefly.

Best action: Jackie has several

■ Jackie makes quick work of a thug in *Twinkle, Twinkle, Lucky Stars*.

fights, including a bout with Dick Wei. However, in his fight with Shoji, Jackie is backed into a corner and is wounded for the final fight. Samo takes out Norton and Kurata, while Yuen gets the third assassin. **Bottom line:** Not as good as its prequel, *My Lucky Stars* (1985). Much of the humor in *Twinkle, Twinkle, Lucky Stars* is in the same vein as *Dumb and Dumber.* Five grown men spend half the movie trying to come up with different ways to have a woman brush up against them or expose flesh. Most of the action scenes are worthwhile.

Rating: 👊👊

■ POLICE STORY

(1985; aka *Police Force*)

Directed by Jackie Chan. Production coordinator Willie Chan. Supervisor Edward Tang. Starring Jackie Chan, Chua Yuen, Brigette Lin Ching Hsia, Bill Tung, Kenneth Tong and Maggie Cheung.

The premise: Jackie is a detective assigned to a team created to bust a highly organized drug ring headed by businessman Chu Tao (played by Chua Yuen). The sting goes horribly wrong, and Jackie sets out to convince Chu's secretary, Selina, to turn in evidence, making her believe that Chu plans to have her killed. Meanwhile, Chu *has* decided that Selina and Jackie should be eliminated and captures Selina, holding her as bait. By the climax of the movie, Jackie is framed for murder and is on the run not only from the criminals, but his former buddies.

Film fact: Jackie was back scripting, starring and directing his own movie. "And boy, let me tell you, it's great to be directing again!" he said, thoughts of Glickenhaus behind him. **Rumor has it:** How many ways can you wreak havoc in a shopping mall? Jackie Chan answers this question with a ten-minute brawl, spectacular stunt work, and so much broken glass that *Police Story* was nicknamed "Glass Story" by the stuntmen who were on the receiving end. **Worst injury:** While trying to stop a hijacked bus, Jackie parks a car in the path of the oncoming vehicle. The highjacker panics and the dri-

ver slams on the brakes, sending the criminals crashing through the front window of the bus and onto the hard pavement just short of the car—which in reality was specially cushioned to break their fall. Because the bus stopped short, the poor guys ate some pavement and ended up in the hospital. Jackie also had a close call when he slid down a thirty-foot pole that was wrapped in a myriad of electric lights. Before the stunt, Jackie wrote in his fan newsletter: "All I have to do is leap from the 6th floor balcony of a shopping arcade onto a giant 30-foot chandelier then slide down on it all the way to the ground. And if glass breaks and sparks fly during the process (and I pray they will because that is the effect I want!), you please pray that I'll still be in one piece when I land on the ground!" Perhaps someone was *praying* instead of doing their *job*—the electricity was supposed to be half voltage. It wasn't. "When I'm coming down, all my skin coming off my hands," Jackie told reporter Mark Caro of the stunt he called his scariest to date. But wait, there's more. Near the beginning of the movie a spectacular car chase was filmed through a hillside shantytown—a construction that cost five hundred thousand Hong Kong dollars. "Four of my boys got badly injured! One had his earlobe cut, another his foot slashed, yet another with a twisted ankle, and, worst of all, the fourth with two broken ribs," Jackie continued. Injuries

■ Opening ceremony for *Police Story II*. That's Papa Chan in the hat.

on *Police Story* were so extensive that many martial artists vowed never to work with Jackie again. "If you saw some of the NG's [mistakes] we didn't use at the end of *Police Story*, I think you'd cry. Lot's of people got hurt, were bleeding, got carried off to the hospital, etc," said Jackie in his newsletter. "I wanted to show all of this, but my boss said it was too much, so we cut it out." **Best action:** *Police Story* was an action groundbreaker. Jackie had set out to show Glickenhaus what *The Protector* (1985) should have been, and he succeeded. Proof? Take into account that no one has paid homage to anything from *The Protector*. Not so *Police Story*. Andrei Konchalovsky took several scenes for *Tango and Cash* (1989), while Brandon Lee lifted the shopping mall motorcycle segment frame by frame for *Rapid Fire*. Don't miss Mars's shining moment as the "assailant" after the damsel in distress. **Jackie says:** "Every time I make an American film, you can tell!" Jackie has prophetically related in many interviews. "*The Protector* and *Police Story* are totally different, and I think *Police Story* is a better movie!" **Note:** August 17, 1985, was Jackie's victory day. That's the day he successfully completed three movies: *Twinkle, Twinkle, Lucky Stars* (1985), *Dragon's Forever* (1987), and *Police Story* (1985). **Bottom line:** The first great modern-day martial arts action picture.

Rating: 🤜🤜🤜🤜🤜

■ ARMOUR OF GOD
(1986; aka *Thunderarm*)

Directed by Jackie Chan. Original story by Edward Tang, Szeto Choek Hoin, Ken Low and John Sheppared. Stunt coordinators Lau Kar Wing and Yuen Chung Heung. Starring Jackie Chan, Alan Tam, Lola Forna and Rosamund Kwan.

The premise: Jackie plays the Asian Hawk, an Indiana Jones–style adventurer, who has recovered an ancient sword. It's bought at auction by Lola Forner (*Wheels on Meals*) after Jackie plants an overzealous bidder in the crowd to jack up the price. Meanwhile, we learn an evil sect, which already has two pieces of a mythical suit of armor of which the sword is part, wants the rest and will stop at nothing to reach their overzealous goal. When they kidnap Jackie's ex-girlfriend—who is now dating his former best friend from the singing group that the three started—it's up to Jackie to infiltrate the cult's mountain lair and fight leather-encased Amazons and habit-clad kickers.

Worst Injury: Chan miscalculated a leap from a castle wall to a tree branch and plummeted headfirst to the ground, hitting a rock and cracking his skull. Today he suffers from permanent partial deafness in one ear and has a thimble-sized hole on the right side of his head. If you ask nice-

■ Jackie in the movie that almost killed him, *Armour of God*.

ly, he'll let you touch it . . . it vibrates when he hums. **Jackie says:** "I didn't concentrate enough. Before that jump I had jumped a long way in *Police Story* (1985), so this seemed to be very easy. The original director Eric Tsang said 'Have you looked at the tree you're jumping to?' and I said, 'Ahh, it doesn't matter.'" He told reporter Bey Logan, "It changed me in that now I'm even more careful. I look on every small stunt as if it's a big stunt. I don't think 'Oh, it's a piece of cake' anymore." Hearing the story of how the Yugoslavian cameraman moved to save the camera instead of saving Chan, interviewer Jonathan Ross from *The Incredibly Strange Film Show* in England asked him, "I wonder where that cameraman is today?" Jackie just smiled. **Rumor has it:** Originally, Jackie had a very short haircut for *Armour of God*. After his operation, he let his hair grow back to its usual length for the completion of the film. "I didn't like that hairstyle. Also, the boss at Golden Harvest (Raymond Chow), will never let me touch my hairstyle again. He thinks that when I cut it I lost my power," Jackie said in *Combat* magazine. **Best action:** A wonderful fight with four femme guards (played half the time by stuntmen and half the time by women—who complained that the suits fit the stuntmen better than they . . . uhm . . . fit them) and the main battle scene inside the cult's mountain-lair dining room. Chan advances the art of kung fu cinema once again. In addition to the clever running joke in which Jackie must break away from the fighting to protect his two friends who just can't seem to find any way out of the place, Jackie invents a new form of fighting that writer Ric Meyers terms "hit and spin." He uses circular attacks and retreats to check his surroundings and the location of the enemy. "It was a brilliant way to explain the sort of ESP kung fu fighters have when surrounded," wrote Meyers. "It also elevated the fight sequence to an amazing dance. This is the scene I will always consider a classic." **Bottom line:** A keeper.

Rating: 🥊🥊🥊🥊

■ NAUGHTY BOYS
(1986)

Chan produced for Golden Way. Jackie has a cameo appearance in a jail scene as the "Big Brother" of the inmates. He also appears in the outtakes.

■ PROJECT A II
(1987)

Directed by Jackie Chan. Screenwriter and producer Edward Tang. Starring Jackie Chan.

After his near-fatal accident, Jackie seemed to realize his own mortality as he went about completing a series of sequels to his successful movies, including this obvious homage to Buster Keaton.

The premise: An epic turn-of-the-century action/comedy. Jackie plays Dragon Ma, the only honest cop in the frontierlike town of Hong Kong on the eve of the 1911 revolution—facing pirates, a corrupt police department, the colonial powers, a desperate imperial government, over-zealous young revolution-aries and the pirates he didn't kill in the first movie. The film offers a perfect synthesis of comedy, drama, motion and a subtle pacifist message.

■ Jackie gets attention in his spiffy duds.

A MOTHER'S LOVE

When he left the China Drama Academy for Australia to join his parents, who were working at the American Embassy, Jackie discovered two things: His parents had been saving for years to buy him a house, and he had an older sister who had since traveled from China to join them.

Although he didn't grow up with his family, Chan has since forged a relationship with them. His father—a distinguished gentleman, usually wearing a Greek sailor's hat and smoking a pipe—can often be seen around Jackie's sets. His mother, however, is a different story.

"For thirty years, my mom is so proud of herself because she has her picture with every American president. She knows every ambassador. Every time I go back, the ambassador says, 'Jackie, don't let your mom go, she takes good care of me.' I say, 'Mom, retire.' She says, 'No, no everybody likes me. I stay here.'

"After that, I became more famous. In all that time, my mom has not seen one of my movies beginning to end. When the fighting starts, she turns around to make coffee or do anything. She just listens. After fighting, she comes back for the comedy things. Then, 'Ha, ha, ha, ha.'

Fighting again, she turns around again. For all those years none of my movies has she seen completely. I remember while doing a stunt on the set once—first time she ever visited me on the set. *Bad* day. As soon as she arrived we had a fighting scene. My mom had never seen my fighting. She was sitting about twenty feet away. BOOM! I get hit in the nose, blood comes out. You know when blood comes out, all my stunt guys, everybody is nervous, 'Quick, quick, get the medicine box. Jackie!' My mom collapsed. Fell down right away. You know what? Next day she goes back to Australia. So all those years, the only worry of my mom is that I get hurt on my head.

"I'll never forget. After I get hurt in Yugoslavia [filming *Armour of God*], seven days later we get the news in Asia—nobody knows. But suddenly one day, Associated Press takes a photo. I think, 'Oh, my God.' I know the news will go to Australia in three days. I call my mom right away. 'Hi mom, how are you?' 'Where are you?' 'Paris.' 'Why are you in Paris?' 'My friend got hurt. Come to see my friends and have a holiday.' 'Okay, see you.' I hang up. Three days later, my mom calls. 'I saw the news, what happened!' 'Ah, company just wanted to do some promotion. It's okay.' Mom says, 'Oh, *scared* me.'

"Of course, later on my mom knows. Two years later, I let the hair grow over the wound, everything looks perfect. I'm going back to see my mom for five days. My mom is always looking at me. The last day, I leave for Hong Kong, my mom cried. 'Jackie, before you go, I want to see your scar. How big is the scar? Where's the hole? The newspapers say you have a hole in your skull.' I said, 'They're all *liars*. Very good operation. Very small.' She looks a *whole* hour, cannot find the hole (pointing to left side of head). I say, 'See, nothing. Good, good doctor.'

"My mom says, 'Ah, now I'm not worried.' She goes away.

"It was the *other* side, not *that* side."

■ Jackie still carries a torch for Rosamund Kwan (and Alan Tam) in *Armour of God*.

Best action: Balletlike fights move at warp speed through a nightclub, a soy-milk-making factory, a fish hatchery and a chicken-plucking establishment. The stunts are also spectacular—especially the tip of the hat to Keaton. In *Steamboat Bill, Jr.*, Buster does a remarkable stunt during a hurricane when a facade falls toward him and he passes safely through a window opening. One inch either way and he would have been nailed into the ground. In *Project A II*, the facade of a ceremonial wall collapses on Chan, who passes safely through a bamboo and paper panel. **Jackie says:** "I spent a lot of money so they [the sets] would not look like sets. All the costumes were imported from England. We had to do extensive research, but I deliberately didn't make the society of nine-

teenth century Hong Kong as bad as it really was. I gave it a healthy look! Supposedly, there was a lot of opium and robberies in the street every day during that period, but I let the audience see mostly nice things," Chan said in his fan publication. "As for the 'pacifist speech' in *Project A II*, in each of my movies I do try to bring a message. Unfortunately, this message is often lost, especially to the Asian audience, who are really only there to see my action." **Rumor has it:** In the film, Jackie fills his mouth with chili peppers, spits on his fists and slaps juice into his opponent's eyes. Guess what? They were real chili peppers. "At the time we shot that scene, I was in a big hurry to finish the movie," Jackie continued. "We had deadlines everywhere from foreign distributors, because you have to send the film to the government one month prior to release. I was working day and night, even doing stunts without rehearsals. We just thought about how the stunts were going to be and did them. Because of the hurry, we didn't have time to make artificial peppers—they had to be the real thing. I tell you, the whole afternoon and night it hurt!" **Bottom line:** With desperate chase scenes, spectacular stunts, humor, suspense, pain and invention, you need more than one viewing to truly appreciate this movie.

Rating: 👊 👊 👊 👊 👊

■ DRAGONS FOREVER
(1987)

Directed by Samo Hung. Starring Jackie Chan, Hung, Yuen Biao, Deanie Yip, Kao Fei, Yuen Wah, Pauline Yeung, Benny "The Jet" Urquidez and Lo Lieh.
Jackie, Yuen Biao and Samo Hung realized they weren't getting any younger, so they came together to do this fight extravaganza advertised as their "farewell" film. Jackie was only thirty-three.

The premise: A widow threatens to take a mobster to court because the chemicals from his illegal drug factory are polluting her fish hatchery. The mobster orders his womanizing lawyer (Chan) to get her to drop her suit, and Chan hires his two buddies—Hung, a good-hearted arms seller, and Biao, a paranoiac technical wizard and sneak-thief—to help out.

Film fact: Bombed horribly at the box office in Japan, a country usually hungry for anything Jackie. **Rumor has it:** Some feel that perhaps a backlash from Samo's declining career at that time caused this movie not to do so well in theaters. **Action:** A rousing fight at the chemical factory featuring an evil-looking Yuen Wah is particularly adrenaline-pumping. Jackie, Samo and Yuen Biao show they still have what it takes, especially Jackie as he once again takes on Benny "The Jet" Urquidez, the bad guys' main coke taster. Look for the kung fu fight stars, such as Dick Wei and the Yuen brothers, guesting throughout. **Bottom line:** Characterization is top-notch. Despite poor showing when released, the film is a pure delight.

Rating: 🖒🖒🖒🖒

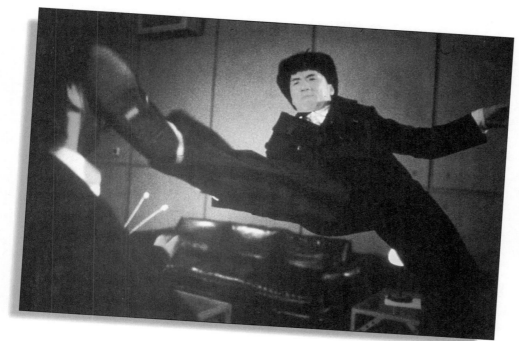

■ "How dare you object to my questioning!" —Jackie as the world's deadliest lawyer in *Dragons Forever.*

THE KEATON SCORECARD

Buster Keaton's motto was "Think slow. Act Fast." Jackie Chan's motto is: "When I do a stunt, I am Buster Keaton." Nothing proves that better than looking at a few of the scenes, props and obstacles that the two have in common on our unofficial scorecard.

■ Jackie takes on a bus and a water spout . . . as well as Vincent Lyn (t, r) and Ken Lo (b-l, r).

BUSTER:

Buster fights swordfish underwater.
—*The Navigator* (1924)

Buster walks against the force of a hurricane.
—*Steamboat Bill, Jr.* (1928)

Buster escapes being crushed by fitting into the window frame of a falling facade.
—*Steamboat Bill, Jr.*

Buster jumps down the decks of a steamboat.
—*Steamboat Bill, Jr*

Buster is chased while tied to a man.
—*Convict 13* (1920)

Buster hangs from the back of a cab.
—*The Cameraman* (1928)

More than one Buster appears on screen at one time.
—*The Playhouse* (1921)

Buster uses a ladder to escape by vaulting over a fence.
—*Cops* (1922)

Buster is injured by a steam train watering spout.
—*The General* (1927)

Buster has a fight atop a moving train.
—*The General*

JACKIE:

Jackie fights sharks underwater.
—*First Strike* (1996)

Jackie walks against the force of a wind tunnel.
—*Operation Condor* (1990)

Jackie escapes being crushed by fitting into the window frame of a falling ceremonial facade.
—*Project A II* (1987)

Jackie jumps down the decks of a cruise ship.
—*City Hunter* (1993)

Jackie is chased while handcuffed to a criminal.
—*Project A II* (1987)

Jackie hangs from the back of a bus.
—*Police Story* (1985)

More than one Jackie appears on screen at one time.
—*Twin Dragons* (1991)

Jackie use a ladder to escape by vaulting over a fence.
—*Project A II* (1987)

Jackie is injured while hanging from a train spout.
—*Supercop* (1992)

Jackie has a fight atop a moving train.
—*Supercop*

■ Catching a ride in
Police Story II.

■ POLICE STORY II
(1988)

Directed by Jackie Chan. Starring Jackie Chan, Maggie Cheung and Bill Tung.

The premise: Two movies in one, with Jackie back as his intrepid Hong Kong cop character. Plotline number one involves the villain from the first movie, who is diagnosed with only a few months to live. He vows to break every bone in Jackie's body during his remaining time on earth, which leads to two great fights—one in a restaurant and one on a playground. Plotline number two involves a team of arsonists terrorizing a major corporation. What do they want? Loads of cash. If the company does not comply, their large holdings—shopping centers, hotels—will be bombed. Only Jackie can save the day, not to mention his kidnapped girlfriend.

Film fact: *Police Story II* won the award for best fight choreography at the Hong Kong Film Awards. **Rumor has it:** This was more or less Chan's *Lethal Weapon*, with him in the Mel Gibson role. **Best action:** Normal people wait for a green light to cross a street. Not Jackie. In *Police Story II* Jackie stands on a balcony, then jumps onto a truck going one way, then a double-decker bus going the other way, dodges two outcropping signs, only to go through a billboard on the second floor of the villain's headquarters. In another fight Chan goes from park to playground, methodically taking out a dozen attackers. **Worst injury:** Jackie had a rather close call while filming *Police Story II*, which he related in his fan club newsletter. "I almost got killed," he said. In one scene, he had to rush into a restaurant for a fight [most people just have lunch] after first crossing the busy highway. "We didn't get permission to film this. We just went out at four in the morning with all our cars and drivers. I didn't know which cars were ours and which were people going to work," Jackie said, as reported in *M.A.M.A.* magazine. The one that ran over him was one of his own, pushing him ten feet down the street. If Jackie had slipped or lost his balance, he would have gone under the vehicle *Indiana Jones*–style without the benefit of special effects. "He kept stopping too soon," Jackie said. "I told him, 'Reach me, then hit your brakes!' Finally, he did." When Jackie was asked what he said to the driver after the shot, he replied, "Good job!" Jackie suffered a head injury while crashing through a billboard and a glass window. Maggie Cheung sustained a horseshoe-shaped gash just above her hairline. Shooting was delayed while she was stitched together. **Bottom line:** "Good job" could also be said to Jackie for this sequel. It achieves heights of delirium with realistic action and some interesting sets, topped off by a fantastic exploding factory with Jackie clearly running from the precariously close airborne molten rubble.

Rating: 👊 👊 👊 👊

■ INSPECTOR WEARS SKIRTS
(1989)

Producer and fight choreographer. (A lunatic *Police Academy* featuring women.)

BRINGING BACK BIAO

Not enough has been written about Yuen Biao. That's a shame, because his talent is just as impressive as his two opera school "brothers" from the China Drama Academy—Jackie Chan and Samo Hung.

■ Brothers Forever—Yuen Biao (l), Samo Hung (c) and Jackie (r) in *Dragons Forever*.

Yuen is the youngest of the three, and started his career with the persona of a perky, slightly smarmy teen idol type that he has traces of even today. He appeared with his two old friends in a string of movies such as *Wheels on Meals* (1984), *Project A* (1984) and *Dragon's Forever* (1987), all of which were hits in varying degrees and all of which show a Yuen Biao that is possibly even more acrobatic than Jackie himself. Look how they complement each other in *Young Master*.

Though not as adventuresome in the outrageous stunt department as Chan, Biao is frighteningly flexible and seemingly able to defy gravity. According to *Film Threat Video Guide*, "Biao's high kick is so amazing he can kick a man standing behind him in the face without even so much as turning around."

Perhaps not wanting to constantly be in the shadows of his towering brothers, Biao moved on to star in some formidable hits of his own, including *Once Upon a Time in China, Pea-*

cock King and *Prodigal Son*. These days, he prefers to keep a low profile and spend time with his family, usually only accepting minor roles in other people's films.

"Yuen was a success, but when he left Golden Harvest he followed the wrong road," explains Jackie to one reporter. "When they [Samo Hung and Biao] have success at Golden Harvest, all the production buyers came out, gave them a blank check. They think they are success . . . not just you . . . not just me, but all of us and Golden Harvest [think that]. Then Samo and Yuen Biao go out and make their own company. So now they [distributors] just buy one Yuen Biao movie, and they don't promote it. Then when Yuen Biao goes down, they say, 'Ah, he's finished.' It's back to Golden Harvest for them.

"So, as soon as they were down, Golden Harvest would not let me make a movie with Yuen Biao anymore," Jackie said in one interview. "We have a tradition, when people's luck is going down—you never go to them. You wait it out. I hate these kinds of traditions. This is why I say, 'Okay, Samo is back.' And then later, I bring Yuen Biao back. Then all three brothers will be together again."

Magic moments have been few and far between these past few years since Jackie, Yuen and Samo made *Dragons Forever*. However, the audience at the 1994 Hong Kong Film Awards got to see a little of the old camaraderie—and the sibling relationship—between these men when they formed a boyish trio to present a Lifetime Achievement Award to Golden Harvest head Raymond Chow. That, coupled with Linda Lee's acceptance speech in Cantonese for her late husband Bruce's Lifetime Achievement Award, made it a shining night to remember.

■ ROUGE
(1988)

Produced by Chan's production company, Golden Way. Directed by Stanley Kwan and starring Anita Mui.

Film Fact: One of Hong Kong's most critically acclaimed films and moneymakers. It won three Golden Horse awards for best actress, cinematography and art direction—worthy of this beautiful film that tells a classic love story through fifty years. The "Madonna" of Hong Kong, Anita Mui, gives a stunning performance. **Jackie says:** "Actually, we decided to make this film because we wanted to prove that our company, Golden Way, apart from making action movies, can make other types of award-winning films as well, and this film has certainly been nominated and in some instances actually won awards in film festivals all over the world," said Chan in his fan publication.

Rating: 🥊 🥊 🥊 🥊 🥊 for drama

■ Film and singing superstar Anita Mui (l) in *Rouge*.

■ PAINTED FACES
(1988)

Coproduced by Golden Harvest and Shaw Brothers Studios. Produced by Mona Fong and Leonard Ho. Written and directed by Alex Law. Starring Samo Hung.

The premise: The Dickensian telling of the China Drama Academy childhoods of Samo Hung, Yuen Biao and Jackie Chan, with Samo starring as their notoriously harsh headmaster, Sifu Yuen. The film starts with a young actor playing Chan entering the school at age seven. His mother can't handle him, and she signs a guardianship paper that is practically slavery, giving the teacher the right to even beat the boy to death. From here we watch the painful development of the young performers until the time their teacher leaves them to go to America.

Film fact: Though Jackie had nothing to do with the making of this movie, it *is* about his life. **Jackie says:** "This film has won quite alot of acclaim, but frankly, personally I don't like it much because I think that it has been glamorized for the screen," said Chan in his newsletter. "A lot of the story is not true. If it were, Samo, Yuen Biao and I would have been much happier kids." **Best action:** This is not a film in which the camera swirls and swoops—it is intimate and quiet. Therefore, it is not motion that is memorable as much as individual images. **Bottom line:** This is a heart-wrenching tale that gives some insight into what makes Chan tick. "*Painted Faces* is a film that gets better the more it's thought about," wrote *Inside Kung Fu* columnist Ric Meyers. "The first half of the movie is reflected and refracted in the second half as Peking Opera traditions go out of style and Hong Kong becomes increasingly westernized. So, although the audience is treated to a condensed, abridged, encyclopedic taste of a decade, director Law crafts each scene so carefully that the overall effect is of excellence."

Rating: 👊👊👊👊👊 for drama

■ MIRACLE
(1989; aka *The Chinese Godfather*, aka *Mr. Canton and Lady Rose*)

Directed, written and choreographed by Jackie Chan. Starring Jackie Chan, Anita Mui, Gloria Yip, Jacky Cheung and Billy Chow.

The premise: A musical/gangster/martial-arts/comic melodrama set in 1930s Hong Kong. Chan is an honest man mistakenly elevated to criminal kingpin status and riches after receiving a lucky rose from a flower vendor. He uses his newfound power to open a nightclub that becomes all the rage, as he battles with gangsters who oppose him. When the in-laws of the flower vendor's child come for a visit, Jackie decides to convince them that she is a refined lady as payback for her kindness.

Film fact: A set was built for *Miracle* at the old Shaw Brothers Studios in Hong Kong, actually requir-

■ Jackie (c) taking care of business in *Miracle*.

ing that part of a mountain be knocked down for the right shot. "You see, I wanted this movie to look totally realistic. I wanted the audience to fantasize too. A movie is always a dream maker—let them go to the cinema, forget everything and just feel good," Jackie said. **Jackie says:** "I remember seeing *Pocketful of Miracles* when my English wasn't so good. I understood the story line, that's all, so I had someone translate it for me. Wow! I loved

it and always kept the idea of making my own version in the back of my mind," Jackie recalled in *Hong Kong Film Connection*. "I used to bring this idea up at meetings and show them the original movie, and the main point of criticism was this: 'What? No fighting?' Finally, we sat down and came up with new ideas to change the film's plot, add fighting and so forth. I added a lot of new things." **Best action:** "I had to think of new stunts. For example, if rope had been used in another movie, it was my job to think of something fresh. We always had to think of funny things as well, not just punches, but fighting that was funny," Jackie continued. That attention to detail paid off in the stairwell scene—which is one of the greatest moments in all of Jackie's movies—as he dodges rickshaws and other obstacles. All four fights in the movie are well conceived and demonstrate Jackie's style of circular fighting, but not as much as the finale in the rope factory when Jackie dances with wrapping hemp, rolling barrels and flying bodies. **Rumor has it:** *Miracle* took nine months to shoot and cost sixty-four million Hong Kong dollars. *Police Story II* (1988) had been scheduled for an early release under Jackie's nose. He was determined to avoid this with *Miracle*, as he explained in his newsletter. "It was supposed to have been finished by Chinese New Year [February], but when I heard that, every day I took only one shot to let Golden Harvest know that it was impossible to get it done by then. Still *Miracle* was rush, rush, rush at the end too. I didn't want to push up the release date because I'd spent so much money already. Finally, the release date was postponed and I had lots of time—I thought. A typhoon came and destroyed my sets and we had to remake them." **Worst injuries:** Jackie ended up with a piece of bamboo between his eye and eyebrow, and a gash on his brow from a misdirected ax handle (he was going backward over a rickshaw at the time). Nothing unusual. But real tragedy did strike—the death of a crew member. News reporters grabbed on like pit bulls, claiming a stuntman had died. In fact, a prop crew member fell off one of the set's buildings. The film's associate producer said that Jackie closed the production down and saw to the welfare of the man's family, which he is probably doing even today. **Will you like it?:** With its subtle tracking shots, elegant montages and witty use of the wide screen, *Miracle* is a winner. Some may find the slapstick overdone, but no more so than scenes between dance routines in a Gene Kelly movie. Of all his films, Jackie probably had his most passionate love affair with *Miracle*. Chances are that you will like it too.

Rating: 👊 👊 👊 👊 👊

■ ARMOUR OF GOD II: OPERATION CONDOR
(1990; aka *Project Eagle*)

Directed by Jackie Chan. Starring Jackie Chan, Eva Cobo, DoDo Cheng, Vincent Lyn, Ken Lo and Shoko Ikeda.

Jackie was no longer the new guy on the block. The pressure was on for a hit. After the success of Golden Harvest's *Teenage Mutant Ninja Turtles*, Team Chan decided the time was right for a movie to appeal to the American market. But producers told him that American cinemas would never screen an all-Asian film, so Jackie decided to do this sequel to his most successful movie, *Armour of God*, with a mostly Caucasian cast.

The premise: Jackie, as the "Asian Hawk," leads a mission in search of a huge cache of gold hidden in the desert by German soldiers during World War II (an idea inspired by Italian actor Aldo Sambrell, seen in many Clint Eastwood movies). A Chinese historian, an accident-prone

CHAN'S BEST STUNTS

Jackie Chan's stunts might elicit this response: the viewers sit motionless, perhaps clutching their seats; simultaneously their eyes bulge and their bottom jaws drop; this is usually followed by sighs of disbelief accompanied by an almost inaudible "This guy is crazy" or "I can't believe he did that." That's just the reaction that Jackie wants. His stunts are thrilling because he's actually doing them. Here are his best examples.

1. *Police Story:* The stakeout sequence beginning *Police Story* is a wonderful ten minutes in action cinema. It begins with a car chase through a hillside shantytown and culminates with Jackie hanging from a bus by the handle of his umbrella.

2. *Police Story:* Jackie slides down a thirty-foot pole wrapped with a myriad of electric lights. He burns the skin off his hands.

3. *Project A:* Taking his inspiration from Harold Lloyd's *Safety Last,* Jackie re-creates the famous hanging-from-the-clock-face routine, only Jackie falls through several awnings and lands headfirst. He is injured on the first take. He does two more!

4. *Police Story II:* Chan somersaults from a moving bus

■ Jackie does Harold Lloyd.

and crashes through a billboard and a factory window. He suffers head injuries.

5. *Police Story III: Supercop:* Jackie jumps from a building onto a helicopter rope ladder, and then proceeds to swing around the heights of Kuala Lumpur, through a billboard and into a steeple, then landing on a moving train. Piece of cake—as long as you can hang on.

6. *Operation Condor:* Taking his inspiration from Buster Keaton's *Steamboat Bill, Jr.,* Chan sets a fight in a wind tunnel that is preceded by fisticuffs on moving metal bellows and a giant oil tank.

7. *Project A II:* Jackie's re-creation of classic Buster Keaton stunts adds charm to this already fun epic. Especially pay attention to the falling ceremonial wall.

8. *Winners and Sinners:* Jackie roller-skates over a Volkswagen bug and under a thundering eighteen-wheeler.

9. *Dragon Lord:* The bun pyramid sporting event can be called a stunt, as over a hundred stuntmen clamber over each other to climb a bamboo tower, until the tower topples and splinters, sending debris and bodies to the ground.

10. *Drunken Master II:* Jackie proves he's still hot by skimming across a bed of hot coals and shooting flames from his mouth.

■ That magnificent man and his flying with ease.
Supercop (t)
Operation Condor (l)

German heiress, and a Japanese ethnologist are in tow as Jackie takes on an assortment of mercenaries with his lightning-fast moves and spy gadgets.

Film fact: Filmed in the Moroccan Sahara desert, Spain, the Philippines and Hong Kong with a ninety-million-Hong-Kong-dollar budget, this was Chan's most expensive feature to date. The most elaborate sets were a Moroccan-style hotel costing one and a half million Hong Kong dollars, and a huge sound stage and wind tunnel built on the old Shaw Brothers Studios lot in Hong Kong. **Rumor has it:** Some "prop" money was taken off the set in Morocco and circulated outside as the real thing. Jackie was summoned to the police station for questioning. The authorities detained the film footage and it was only after involving lawyers from Britain, Hong Kong and Morocco that the footage was safely flown back to Jackie in Hong Kong. On a humorous—and touching—note, Jackie apparently forbade all the cast and crew to eat the fruit baskets in their hotel rooms. Why? He had been told on a previous trip that most of the kids in Morocco are so poor that they have never tasted fruit. Chan distributed the fruit to every child he saw that day. **Worst injuries:** Jackie suffered a bleeding chest after he was kicked forty-three times in a series of retakes for one scene. However, the Jackie Chan Stuntmen's group took the biggest blow. After ten years, Jackie decided to disband his group after this movie, only using old regulars on a movie-by-movie basis. This was attributed to infighting among the group as to who was the leader. But it has also been rumored that some of the members were believed to have triad ties and were feeding information to their bosses. Disbanding was a convenient way to eliminate the infiltrator. **Jackie says:** The Sahara led to major problems. "There were sandstorms during which it was impossible to work!" Jackie said in his fan publication. "Camels didn't want to obey! We didn't have enough water for the crew and the actors! And I was about to forget scorpions coming each night to visit us! A member of the crew was bitten by one of them, but he was saved because we were lucky enough to have a doctor with us. We didn't have time to get bored in the desert!" Vincent Lyn, hanging on a wire, was also hurt on the wind tunnel set when he was slammed against a wall so hard that he lost consciousness. **Best action:** The comic bout between Jackie, Ken Lo and American martial artist Vincent Lyn in a wind tunnel inspired by a Mitsubishi auto testing facility and Buster Keaton's *Steamboat Bill, Jr.* **Bottom line:** A story that seems to have gotten out of hand, the most insulting part being the three female stars sharing the same brain, who are there only to represent the three markets Golden Harvest wanted to capture—Japanese, Chinese and Western. Often called a Chan latter-day low point, there are still comic moments to be had.

Rating: ✊✊✊✊

■ ISLAND ON FIRE
(1991)

Produced by Jimmy Wang Yu. Starring Jackie Chan, Tony Leung, Andy Lau and Samo Hung.

The premise: In the Hong Kong of the future, Jackie plays a pool shark whose girlfriend is brutally stabbed by a vengeful rival. Apparently hospitals of the future won't operate without money up front, so in order to save his love's life, Jackie wins at cards but must kill the angry loser to get out of the club in one piece. He ends up in jail, where Samo Hung, Tony Leung (*The Lover*) and pop singer/actor Andy Lau are also interred because of their own touching tales. The film enters *La Femme Nikita* territory when Chan, Hung, Leung and Lau are recruited for a dangerous mission outside the prison. Before ya know what's hit ya, the four man hit squad is taking on what appears to be the entire Filipino army.

Film fact: *Cool Hand Luke* meets *The Wild Geese*. *Island on Fire* was produced in record time—possibly because everyone in the movie was in debt to Jimmy Wang Yu—and features a homage to almost every prison movie ever made. (This was despite the fact that an Iraqi war interrupted filming and the cast and crew had to stay in the Philippines for months.) **Rumor has it:** This was Jackie's second film for triad boss Jimmy Wang Yu. When asked why by writer Bey Logan, Chan said, "Very hard to explain. . . . I have to make it because Wang Yu ask me . . . he helped me a great deal when I had problems with the Chinese Mafia. To play in the movie was good way to repay him because my name helped him to sell the movie in a lot of countries." **Jackie says:** Jackie is vocal about his feelings on *Island on Fire*, calling it "rubbish." "All those years he [Wang Yu] was a very big star before," Chan also told Logan. "He was the biggest action star in Asia. After, he was not doing so good. He kind of watched me growing up. When I go to the set, I really want to do something for him," Jackie told *Hong Kong Film Comment*. "But when I look around beside me, all his friends are just fooling around. Even the director fooling around. Then, just by myself, I cannot do anything. I'm just standing there, just fooling around also." **Best action:** An exhilarating fight against a druglord's militia ends the film and, you should be warned, Jackie's character. But the two Andy Lau fights—one in a casino and one in the jail—precede this grimness and are worthwhile. **Bottom line:** Jackie's face is prominent on the video sleeve of this movie, and although his part *is* sizable, he is not the star. It's amazing he found time to do as much as he did, since he was directing and starring in the problematic *Operation Condor* (1990) simultaneously. Just more proof of Wang Yu's influence. All considered, *Island on Fire* isn't that bad. It does have some surprisingly good moments and a haunting score.

Rating: 👊👊

■ TWIN DRAGONS
(1991; aka *Dragon Duo*)

Directed by Tsui Hark and Ringo Lam. Starring Jackie Chan, Teddy Robin-kwan, Maggie Cheung, Nina Li-chi, Philip Chan, David Chiang, Anthony Chan, Alfred Cheung, Wang Lung Wei, Liu Chia Liang, Tsui Hark, Ringo Lam, Wong Jing, Eric Tsang, Chu Yuen, Jacob Cheung, Ng See Yeun, Kirk Wong, John Woo and more.

The premise: Jackie Chan and . . . *Jackie Chan* are cast as identical twin brothers separated at birth. One baby, Wan Ming, is "adopted" by a loving town drunk and grows up to become an auto mechanic and illegal car racer. The other twin, Ma Yu, raised by his natural parents, immigrates to the United States and becomes a concert pianist and conductor. Twenty-eight years later, Wan Ming and his buddy, Tarzan, are in trouble with crooks to the tune of $300,000 when in steps Ma Yu, performing his first-ever concert in Hong Kong (shades of Van Damme's *Double Impact*, only better). Adding to the fun is the fact that what one twin does affects the other. Throw in some confused girlfriends to complete the picture.

Film fact: Long passed are the days when Jean-Claude Van Damme was in Hong Kong begging Jackie Chan to let him be in one of his movies. He pretty much has his own leg to stand on—and kick with—now. And it seems that whatever controversy existed about the two megastars making similar movies—Van Damme's *Double Impact*

■ What did you say about her hair?—Jackie as one of the twins in *Twin Dragons*.

and Jackie's *Twin Dragons*—has evaporated, especially since Jackie visited Tsui Hark, Dennis Rodman and Jean-Claude on the Italy-based set of *Double Team* in 1996. You have to wonder, with both Van Damme and Chan showing Dennis a few martial arts moves, if Rodman's pink boa kept getting in the way. Hmmm. . . . **Rumor has it:** Produced as a charity cash cow so the Hong Kong Directors Guild could build a new headquarters, more than eighty actors and directors appear in the film. Though the movie did well, at the time of this writing the new headquarters has yet to go up. **Jackie says:** "Very hard. Every scene with the twins, we have to shoot twice. One time, I play one twin. Different hair. Different clothes. Then we keep the camera the same place, I go and change, then I play the other twin. Very confusing! I'm all the time thinking: 'Who am I now?'" he said in *Martial Arts Illustrated*. He also told *Hong Kong Film Comment*, "I want to try to understand what is the special effect. Right now I think in Asia, Tsui Hark is best known for special effects. So this is why I want to learn from him, to see what's going on. But I was very surprised and disappointed. Compared to Hollywood special effects, *Twin Dragons* is shit! After that, I'm totally disappointed about the whole Hong Kong special effects. This is why I'm not doing special effects anymore, except with people from Hollywood." **Best action:** The finale at a Mitsubishi car testing facility is a real crowd pleaser, and one that will surely merit a rewind. At one point in the fight, Jackie falls to the ground, rolling underneath a car that is being held up by two hydraulic lifts. His adversaries release the car and it falls to the floor, barely missing Jackie as he rolls underneath. Just as he's getting to his feet, another car is released from a ramp. Jackie jumps on the moving car and runs over the top as it rolls beneath him. The slightest miscalculation could have meant disaster. **Bottom line:** *Twin Dragons*, while not liked by many Chan fans, nor by Jackie himself, *is* charming.

    Rating: 👊👊👊👊

■ POLICE STORY III: SUPERCOP
(1992)

Directed by Stanley Tong. Screenplay by Tang King–Sung, Ma Mei–Ping and Lee Wei–Yee. Starring Jackie Chan, Michelle Kahn, Maggie Cheung, Tsang Kong, Yuen Wah and Lo Lieh.

The premise: Jackie Chan, the self-styled "supercop" from his first two installments of the *Police Story* series, goes to China to cooperate with the authorities in cracking an international drug ring. His partner for this mission is the no-nonsense, two-fisted Director Wang (played with aplomb by Michelle Kahn—aka Michelle Yeoh—of *Yes, Madam, Wing Chun* and *Heroic Trio*) of the grim People's Republic Army. Their

■ Jackie Chan and the fabulous Michelle Kahn in *Police Story III: Supercop*.

MUST-SEE MOVIES

New Chan fan? Don't know where to start? Here are the movies that can't be missed:

1. *Police Story:* Chan is out to capture a druglord, but his lead witness is kidnapped and Jackie is accused of murder. The show-stopper is the downhill crash through the shantytown.

2. *Project A:* Dragon Ma (Chan) must stop a notorious pirate in the South China Sea. Daring fights don't pull any punches.

3. *Drunken Master:* An oldie but goodie based loosely on the life of legendary martial artist Wong Fei Hung. Heinous training/torture rituals, and Jackie's ability to endure, never cease to please.

4. *Drunken Master II:* A sequel that stands on its own. See the finale to believe it.

5. *Armour of God:* Jackie à la Indiana Jones as the Asian Hawk. His ex-girlfriend is kidnapped by greedy religious fanatics, and it's up to Jackie to save both her and her new boyfriend, who happens to be his ex-best friend. Harrison Ford hasn't done that one yet.

6. *Project A II:* A Keatonesque sequel, complete with Jackie's lunch of red hot chili peppers.

7. *Police Story II:* Jackie has firecrackers flung at his torso, aptly proving that he who plays with fire gets burned. Once again, girlfriend gets kidnapped.

8. *Police Story III: Supercop:* Chan is out to trap the mother of all druglords—the elusive Chaibat. And yes, you guessed it, the girlfriend gets kidnapped. Michelle Kahn does duty as the *real* woman.

9. *Miracle:* Jackie tries to pass off a flower vendor as a refined lady. Hong Kong songstress Anita Mui (*Drunken Master II, Rouge, Heroic Trio*) stands in for the love interest.

10. *Wheels on Meals:* A pickpocket with a heart of gold is kidnapped and Jackie, Yuen Biao and Samo Hung come to the rescue.

11. *Armour of God: Operation Condor:* The Asian Hawk must find a hidden cache of Nazi gold in the Sahara desert. Just to complicate matters, his *three* female partners get kidnapped.

12. *Crime Story:* Jackie takes on a dramatic role in this true story of a businessman who is kidnapped . . . twice.

■ Jackie in *Police Story III: Supercop*.

undercover activities take them from a prison in Canton to the Thailand jungle to the main streets of Malaysia, as they try to pin down the elusive druglord Chaibat.

Film fact: For the first time in a Cantonese film, at the urging of director Stanley Tong, Jackie uses his own voice for sync sound instead of having a voice dubbed in later. This greatly adds to his overall performance, giving us an authentic tone that fits his character. Plus, Jackie's dream finally came true: He won the Best Actor Award for this film at the Golden Horse Awards in Taiwan—a first for an action film star. **Kahn says:** Kahn, in her comeback film after a divorce from producer Dickerson Poon, was giving *Supercop* her considerable all. Thus, Kahn, a former ballet dancer, wanted to do her own stunts—including riding a motorcycle onto a moving train. "When I see the movie now, I sit there and think I must have been mad," she says. **Rumor has it:** Fred Dannen of the *New Yorker* wrote that Jackie sat glumly by the side of the train during filming of this stunt after trying to talk Michelle out of doing it. The inference was that Jackie didn't want to be bested. However, Michelle says that Jackie is like a big brother to her and was just concerned. **Best action:** Chan himself, undoubled, dangles on a ladder from a careening

helicopter as it swoops through the obstacle course that is downtown Kuala Lumpur. Film critic David Chute wrote that it's the sheer foolhardy intensity of Jackie Chan's eagerness to please that is breathtaking in this scene. Would Schwarzenegger go this far, literally risking life and limb to give his audience a better stunt thrill? Michelle Kahn is incredible in her action scenes, providing a refreshing change as a woman in a Jackie Chan movie who is more than window dressing. **Jackie says:** "There were hundreds of spectators who came by foot, by car, by bicycle, all drawn by the novelty of seeing a film in progress," said Jackie in his monthly newsletter. "Now I know how an animal in a zoo feels!" **Worst injury:** "It was a boat chasing scene and we were shooting beyond Clear Water Bay in very rough seas and I got properly seasick!" continued Jackie. "In fact, ever since I had my brain operation in Yugoslavia, I've had this severe seasick problem. I don't know the actual medical term, but it's got something to do with the fluid level in the ears." **Bottom line:** *Supercop* has wonderful moments and spectacular stunts. It also has the closest thing Jackie has ever had to a political statement in one of his movies. Jackie's character jokes to Kahn's mainland Chinese inspector that it doesn't matter which government gets the bad guys' loot, since 1997 is just around the corner, when Hong Kong is no longer a British colony. That thought aside, this is one good movie. **Note:** *Supercop* was the first film released in 1996 under Jackie's deal with Miramax, with passable dubbing (Jackie and Michelle did their own) and a better sound track than the original (although "Kung Fu Fighting" is a bit insulting). Legitimate laser discs are out there, courtesy of Miramax.

Rating: 👊👊👊👊

■ ONCE UPON A TIME IN CHINA II
(1992)

Jackie sings the theme song, which is a classically heroic tune with words about being the best man and fighter possible.

■ ACTRESS
(1993; aka *Center Stage*)

Produced by Jackie Chan. Directed by Stanley Kwan. Starring Maggie Cheung.

The beautiful and tragic true story of a famous Hong Kong actress who is so beaten down by the attentions of the press that she commits suicide. Award winner.

Rating: 👊👊👊👊👊 for drama

■ CITY HUNTER
(1993)

Directed by Wong Jing. Starring Jackie Chan, Gary Daniels, Richard Norton, Chingmy Yau Shuk-ching, Joey Wang, Kumiko Goto, Leon Lai and Michael Wong.

The premise: Jackie is "City Hunter" Ryu Saeba, based on the popular Japanese *manga* (comic book) and *anime* (cartoon) character of the same name. In the movie, as in the comic, Ryu is a womanizing, perpetually hungry P. I. who, along with Kaori (Joey Wang), his dead partner's cousin, takes on a case to retrieve Kiuyoko (Kumiko Goto), the rebellious runaway daughter of a Japanese newspaper tycoon. Shades of Steven Seagal's *Under Siege*, as Jackie follows the runaway onto a cruise ship that has also been earmarked by a group of terrorists led by Richard Norton.

Film fact: *City Hunter* began filming before Jackie even had time to breathe after wrapping *Supercop*. **Rumor has it:** When Golden Harvest announced that it had bought the rights and would be filming *City Hunter* with Jackie, everyone was stunned that he would be playing a pervert, as per the *manga* character. That wasn't, isn't and has never been Jackie's style. Serious character changes were made for the big screen, and perversions were toned down, leaving the action and comedy intact. **Jackie says:** It's common knowledge that Jackie himself didn't like this movie, as he clearly

showed in a *Hong Kong Film Connection* interview. "Wong Jing . . . ah, *City Hunter* . . . the director really has the responsibility. I hate when they [directors] cheat. From the beginning, they say, 'Jackie we'll do this, Jackie we'll do that.' But later on, when they are filming . . . they try to cut corners to get the next contract. I hate that. It is so easy to believe people." **Best action:** In the surreal parody of the video game *Street Fighter II*, a heavily made-up Chan becomes several of the game's characters including the huge sumo wrestler "E. Honda" and the female "Chun Li," as he battles Gary Daniels as the blond muscleman "Ken." In another scene, Chan sends a hilarious tip of the hat to Bruce Lee in his takeoff on the fight between Lee and Kareem Abdul-Jabbar from *Game of Death*. Cornered by two giants in the ship's theater, Bruce himself is on screen giving Jackie an idea or two on how to deal with the behemoths—of course, translated into the Chan style. **Worst injury:** Jackie hurt his leg while performing a skateboarding stunt in which he was being chased down a hill by a group of skateboarding teens. Although the stunt seemed simple, he fell and spent time in a wheelchair and on crutches. **Bottom line:** This is one of those movies that Chan fans either like or hate. Aside from an ill-advised musical number, it's a lark!

Rating: 👊 👊 👊

■ PROJECT S
(1993; aka *Once a Cop: Supercop II*)

Directed by Stanley Tong. Cameo by Jackie Chan (in drag) as an undercover cop tracking a transvestite jewelry thief. Starring Michelle Kahn.

Film Fact: A sequel to *Supercop* (1992), with Michelle playing her same character from her first teaming with Chan. Jackie is also playing his same character, but his path never crosses Michelle's, and his cameo has nothing to do with the main plot. Jackie says, 'I had no choice but to do it. The studio asked me, and I owe them a lot.' *Project S* is a good movie, with Michelle giving her high-octane all.

Rating: 👊 👊 👊

■ CRIME STORY
(1993)

Directed by Kirk Wong. Starring Jackie Chan, Kent Cheng, Poon Ling-ling, Ng Wing-mie, Blackie Ko Shou-liang, Stephen TK Chan, Lo Wai-kwong, Chung Fa and Mars.

The premise: Based on the true story about a businessman who was kidnapped twice and held for a ransom of $6 million. Jackie plays the police detective in charge of the case, who is going though relationship problems and mood swings of his own, as he fails to keep those around him from harm. It's almost an autobiographical moment when the villain is trapped under rubble in a building that is about to explode. He tells Jackie that he thinks he is crazy, that he tries too hard, that he never gives up. Basically, that he should stop trying to dig him out. Jackie's only reply is to say that this is the way he is, and continue to desperately try to save the villain as well as a trapped child. **Film fact:** The Walled City—a longtime criminal safe haven in Hong Kong—was being demolished as this film was in production. Chan utilized the planned explosions for this volatile movie. **Rumor has it:** Jet Li had originally been cast as the lead in *Crime Story*, but the murder of his triad manager by other triads caused him to back out and retreat to China for a time. Chan picked up the reins. Director Wong expressed concern about the schedule, fearing that because of Jackie's busy schedule and filming three movies at once, this movie wouldn't hold up. It does, though certainly not Kirk's vision of it. **Jackie says:** *"Crime Story* came about when I was making *Twin Dragons* (1991)," said Chan in his newsletter. "Kirk Wong was always talking about this project because he wanted to get my opinion. I thought the story was very good. Afterwards I found out the chosen actor didn't have time to make his movie. If he couldn't find another actor, the script would be postponed. I know the director needed a change and he also had to make a living. I told my boss that I wanted to make this movie to help the director, plus I was

curious about this genre." Hating this movie passionately at first, Jackie's opinion has mellowed over time. "I try to stretch a little," he said recently to reporter Jawas Illavia. "I did cop films before, but always cop comedy, like *Police Story* (1985). This movie is based on real events, on real problems we have here in Hong Kong. It's very serious. Many of my older fans don't like it. It's good to always try new things, though. I like *Crime Story*. I think, as time goes by, people will like it more." **Accident:** While rushing to finish *Crime Story*, one of the sets on the Golden Harvest studio lot caught fire. Fortunately, Jackie and the cast were taking a break when the incident occurred. The fire was blamed on the cigarette butt of a negligent crew member, and the set took around two million Hong Kong dollars to rebuild. It's surprising that there weren't more serious accidents while trying to give birth to this overdue baby (two years). Crew and cast alike worked in thirty-six-hour nonstop stretches trying to wrap and meet deadline so Jackie could start on *Drunken Master II* (1994). **Best action:** Watching the Walled City explode, with Jackie racing through the collapsing buildings, is a pyrotechnics dream and is undoubtedly the best action sequence. **Bottom line:** There's a lot to like here. Check it out.

Rating: 👊👊👊👊

■ DRUNKEN MASTER II

(1994; aka Drunken Monkey II)

Directed by Liu Chia Liang (aka Liu Jialiang, aka Lau Ka-leung) and Jackie Chan. Screenplay by Edward Tang. Starring Jackie Chan, Ti Lung, Anita Mui, Andy Lau, Liu Chia Liang, Mark Houghton, Ken Lo, Louis Roth, Ho Sung Pak, Chin Kar-lok, Bill Tung, Felix Wong and Wong Yat-hwa.

Twenty years after the original blockbuster movie, Jackie once again took on the role of the venerable Wong Fei Hong, but with a few noticeable differences. In *Drunken Master* (1978),

Chan's Wong Fei Hong was a rebellious youth. In *DM II*, he is now a young man faced with maturity and the chance to stand up for his country, while still getting into some hilarious situations with his stern father and fun-loving stepmother.

The premise: A European company is stealing national treasures from China to sell overseas (shades of *Dragon Lord*). A Chinese government agent, played by veteran actor and original director Liu Chia Liang, is sent to investigate the thefts and the trail leads him to Beijing. There he crosses paths with herbalist and kung fu master Wong Kei-Ying (Ti Lung) and his son Wong Fei Hong (Chan), who have come to the capital to buy herbs and medicines. When Liu's luggage is accidentally switched with Chan's, a chain of events begins that engulfs them both.

Film fact: Another "charity" project to help the Hong Kong Stuntman's Guild build a new headquarters. The film grossed over twenty-two million Hong Kong dollars, setting all-time records. No word on whether *that* headquarters was ever built. **Rumor has it:** *DM II* was plagued by production delays—ten months! It was mostly scheduling problems among the actors, but there was also tension on the set between Jackie and Liu Chia Liang (director and star of such classics as *Mad Monkey Kung Fu* and *Legendary Weapons of China*). The latter lost the battle of wills and left the project, taking British bad-guy Mark Houghton (Liang's student) with him. Jackie then served double duty as both the film's director and leading actor while dealing with an ever-increasing budget and a looming 1994 Chinese New Year release date. **Worst injury:** "At the end, I am supposed to fight with a Korean guy [Ho Sung Pak, recognizable as "Liu Kang" in the video games *Mortal Kombat and Mortal Kombat II*]. But this guy, he has no rhythm. After a few shots, he just wants to take a break because his leg cannot continue," Jackie related in *Hong Kong Film Connection*. "Then his leg twists, and he wants to take another two days holiday. I say, 'Just kick. What can you do? Let me know.' He tried very hard, but he just couldn't fin-

ish the movie. So—OUT!" (Ken Lo was brought in for the energetic finale.) Jackie also broke the nose of a French martial artist, who starting yelling at Chan for the accident, informing him he would never work with him again. By all accounts, Jackie's terse reply was, "No. *You* won't." Jackie also sustained burns from a bed of coals, and he and Ken Lo hurt their noses when they butted heads. **Best action:** There are several memorable fights, most notably when director Liu Chia Liang takes on Jackie with fists, spears and swords underneath a train, the station building and a barn. This is matched by the ax-wielding battle at the local teahouse, the climax in a steel foundry and a wonderful moment when Jackie is forced into a street fight. We haven't even mentioned the drunken boxing bout in the town square yet! Whew! **Jackie says:** "This film is very difficult to make, you know! This is the sequel to the film that made me famous, so I have to make this film special—the very best film that I can make, so that people aren't disappointed. It truly gives me a lot of headaches." When asked about the deadline problems, Jackie joked to one reporter, "Fifteen years ago we finish part one . . . maybe in fifteen years time we finish part two!" **Bottom line:** If you aren't a Jackie Chan convert, this movie may make you one. His best film of the nineties.

Rating: 👊👊👊👊👊

■ RUMBLE IN THE BRONX
(1994)

Directed by Stanley Tong. Written by Edward Tang and Fibe Ma. Produced by Barbie Tung and coproduced by Roberta Chow. Executive producer Raymond Chow. Starring Jackie Chan, Anita Mui, Francoise Yip, Bill Tung, Marc Akerstream, Garvin Cros, Morgan Lam and Kris Lord.

The premise: When an off-duty policeman from Hong Kong (Chan), comes to New York City to attend his uncle's wedding, his plans

HIGH-KICKING LO

That high-kicking limb that tries to powder Jackie Chan to charcoal bits at the end of *Drunken Master II* has a torso and a face attached, all belonging to Kenneth Lo. If you haven't heard of him yet, you probably will.

When Chan discovered Lo working as a bouncer at a popular Hong Kong night club in 1988 and hired him as his bodyguard, Ken was already a successful kickboxing champion, and by all accounts a well-liked "doorman" . . . at least by those he didn't throw out. He had never seriously considered a career in the movies, but Jackie would change all that.

"I was very lucky in that Jackie saw me and asked me to be his personal bodyguard," Lo told *Inside Kung Fu.* "And after working with Chan as his bodyguard, Jackie said to me one day, 'Why don't you try to be an actor also, instead of a bodyguard?' And so Jackie put me in one of his movies and that was my first real chance to become an actor."

Born in Laos, Ken became interested in martial arts when he was sixteen starting with tae kwon do. When his parents forbade him to fight, he continued studies in secret, becoming very interested in full-contact fighting and Thai boxing.

His hero then was another Hong Kong actor. "I was very influenced by Bruce Lee," he continued. "He was my hero and it was Bruce Lee that got me interested in taking up the martial arts. I would have liked very much to have met him. But he passed away long before I had a chance to come to Hong Kong."

Since taking Jackie's advice, Lo has slowly been gaining recognition with films outside of Chan's realm and high-profile parts in such Chan movies as *Operation Condor* (1990) and *Drunken Master II* (1994), where he goes *mano-a-mano* with Jackie in the unforgettable finale. He is currently scheduled to be in several upcoming Jackie projects.

"I consider Jackie a great friend," said Ken to interviewer John Little. Lo is Jackie's bodyguard no longer, but he has not forgotten the man who gave him his start, "We do many things together in Hong Kong."

include a little relaxation and sightseeing. But when his uncle sells the family store, Jackie sticks around to help the new owner (Anita Mui) adjust. What Jackie and Anita find out too late—and what the uncle neglects to tell them—is that the store is harassed by a local gang who constantly steals from the business and demands payoffs.

Film fact: *Rumble in the Bronx* was filmed miles away from New

York in Vancouver, Canada. The snow-covered mountain peaks in the background give it away. "When you are filming in the real Bronx, there are a lot of people who throw the bottles at you from the rooftop," explained Jackie to one reporter about why they avoided the Big Apple and environs. So did this odd name choice confuse anyone? "Oh, in Hong Kong we have different title," Chan says. "*Trouble Area.*" **Worst injury:** "Jackie accidentally got run over by a giant hovercraft," said director Stanley Tong in *Inside Kung Fu.* "I dug a hole in the beach for him to jump into. I wanted the hovercraft to barely touch him, so when he falls down, it doesn't look like he's falling into a hole. The first try wasn't too good. It didn't have the right impact. The machine went over him." A hovercraft sucks up fifteen tons of air pressure, so every hole in Jackie's body was packed full of sand. "I tell Jackie to let the hovercraft hit him a bit harder. It did and Jackie flew fifteen feet through the air. He was okay, but it scare me." The second accident was more serious. "I had to jump from a bridge onto a passing hovercraft," said Jackie in the same interview. "After I jump, I landed on the hovercraft and my foot looked like it was folded over. The cameraman looked at me. I said, 'Did you get the shot?' He nods yes. I say, 'Good.'" Jackie was carried off on a stretcher to the nearest hospital after breaking his ankle. Miraculously, he took only one day off from shooting, returning to the set for the last twenty days of filming wearing a sock disguised as a sneaker which he wore over a cast, so that he could continue working. Francoise Yip and two stuntwomen broke legs during the filming of the motorcycle stunts. Not to be outdone, Tong sprained his ankle demonstrating a stunt to Jackie, leaving the movie's two main men in wheelchairs by the time shooting wrapped. **Jackie says:** "This movie? This movie I just broke my ankle and some other things . . . my face . . . real glasses broke on my face . . . my arms . . . some other small things. Small blood, it's okay. I was supposed to chase the boat and start fighting [for the finale]. So, when I broke my leg, we didn't know what to do," related Chan to one writer. "I start thinking, and everyone is like,

'How do we finish this movie?' Then, I went across the street to get a drink and I saw this big Swiss Army knife. I looked at the knife and said, 'Ah, it makes sense.' I can cut the air bag on the hovercraft. Then I went and told Stanley. Then we came up with the car. Lamborghini. Perfect! We spend one hundred and fifty thousand dollars, and I get to drive the car. It works." **Best action:** The showstopper is the gang lair battle when Jackie orchestrates a fight with the rhythm of a Gene Kelly dance routine, using every object around him as a dance partner *and* a weapon. **Bottom line:** If you can ignore the ending, you might like this movie. Even then, it depends on which version you see. *Rumble in the Bronx* was released in the United States via New Line Cinema during 1996. It was released in Asia long before that. The two versions are distinctly different animals. Massive reediting and dubbing were needed to prepare it for stateside audiences, and it made all the difference. Confusing subplots were eliminated, bits of information were added for clarity, and the film was restructured to make Chan's character look more heroic. Seek out the New Line version.

Rating: 👊👊👊👊

■ THUNDERBOLT
(1995)

Directed by Gordon Chan. Starring Jackie Chan, Anita Yuen, Wing-yee, Michael Wong Man-tak, Kayama Yuzo, Eguro Mari, Sawada Kenya, Ken Lo, Chor Yun and Corey Yuen. Stunt director Samo Hung. Car stunt director Frankie Chan.

The premise: A cat-and-mouse plot with Chan chasing illegal car racers through Hong Kong and Tokyo. In between, Jackie is harassed by the crazy, joy riding international criminals and their henchmen who destroy his home and kidnap his sister to lure him into a race.

Film fact: *Thunderbolt* cost a record two billion Hong Kong dollars. "That's the biggest production in Asia," said Jackie. "That's twenty five million dollars in the U.S. In America, I think the cheapest ones cost more

than that." **Jackie says:** "People rave about the action sequences, but frankly, I am not too happy with *Thunderbolt*! I am not saying it is not good but it certainly could have been much better! Without my knowledge, Golden Harvest had booked it for the last summer date all over Asia," Jackie wrote in his fan club magazine. "As a result, I had to rush through it at the end under a lot of pressure. That really made me mad! I don't like to work with deadlines. I want a film to be perfect, every foot of it, before I show it to the audience. It just seems stupid to me after investing so much effort and money in a film, then in the end rush through it just to meet a certain play date. Believe me, I will never let the production company 'bully' me again." **Rumor has it:** The director credit for *Thunderbolt* reads "Gordon Chan," but the movie obviously features recognizable styles. Jackie explained why to journalist Paul Sherman. "We had four units—he [Gordon] had one unit, I had one unit, Samo Hung had one unit. He [Gordon] was the main director. The fighting scenes were Samo. The car chase scenes were Frankie Chan. Some other scenes were by me." **Best action:** Chan takes on a score of Japanese Yakuza and Chinese thugs in a colorful pachinko parlor, where the fighters seem to mimic bouncing balls. It's a powerful Samo-directed encounter, but the best fight occurs in Jackie's car garage. It starts slow and stylized, but builds to a frenzy, never stopping, using camera angles to add to the tension and excitement. **Worst-injury:** While filming *Thunderbolt* in Sendai, Japan, Jackie lost control of the car he was driving during one of the race scenes and was thrown off the track. Later, while filming a car explosion, Jackie was standing so close that his eyebrows were burned. Neither accident caused any serious danger. However, a fall from the container port in Kwai Chung hurt his back and shooting was called off twice in the next week because of the pain. **Bottom line:** This is another one of those films that Chan fans either like or hate, especially considering the final car race reminiscent of *Speed Racer*. It's only the sparse action and Chan's admirable attempt to try something new that saves *Thunderbolt*.

 Rating: 🤜🤜🤜

■ POLICE STORY IV: FIRST STRIKE
(1996)

Director and stunt director Stanley Tong. Screenplay by Stanley Tong, Nick Tramontane, Greg Mellot and Elliot Tong. Starring Jackie Chan, Jackson Lou, Chen-Chun Wu, Jouri Petrov, Bill Tung and Yuri Batchov.

The premise: Jackie is recruited by the CIA to investigate an international arms smuggling operation. When he goes undercover to follow the suspect, a Ukrainian showgirl, all the way to the Black Sea, he is spotted by her partner—an arms dealer who also happens to be a Chinese/Australian ex-CIA agent. The arms dealer and his men are onto Jackie, triggering several skirmishes until a large action set piece on the snow sierras of the Ukraine. Add nuclear bomb threats and great white sharks and you get the picture.

Film fact: The snow scenes were shot five hours out of Melbourne, Australia, at the ski resort of Falls Creek—not in Russia. Chan and his crew of seventy-five were ferried by Sno-Cat to remote locations to film the stunts. Because houses had to be built and the crew accommodated, this scene that takes up twenty minutes on screen cost two million Australian dollars to film. **Rumor has it:** Jackie wanted to call this film *Piece of Cake*, but the title was changed because the consensus was that *First Strike* sounded like a more serious movie. **The action:** The underwater fight with the sharks will elicit a chuckle and a groan, but the ladder fight in which Jackie uses a giant utility ladder as a pole is worthy of Chan. **Jackie says:** "For me, this kind of fighting scene is a piece of cake, but for Hollywood action stuntmen, they say, 'How *can* you do that?'" **Worst injury:** If harm to your psyche can be counted as an injury, then *First Strike* was a doozy. "I haven't had a proper sleep during the past two weeks!" Jackie wrote in his monthly newsletter. "Me and the crew have been working 25 hours a day, trying desperately to complete the underwater shark sequence in Mooloolaba, Australia!" And the sharks that Jackie had to fight were not as "obedient" as

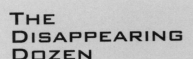

THE DISAPPEARING DOZEN

Sometimes the movies Jackie is rumored to be making, or wants to make, can be just as entertaining as the ones he actually *did* create. A few we'd like to see. The others, well, you decide. . . .

1. *Meeting of the Muscles:* Sly Stallone and Jackie might make a movie together. Stallone flew Chan out for the premier of *Cliffhanger* and to the set of *Demolition Man.* Sly's mom, Jacqueline Stallone, visited Hong Kong to line up the Jackster for *Rambo IV.* **Status:** Little things such as roles and scripts were never ironed out. Jackie wants costar billing. Stallone says he doesn't have the rights to *Rambo IV.* Since the two are friends, anything could still happen, and in fact it has. Now it seems the two will be together in a Joe Eszterhas–penned movie to be directed by Arthur Hiller entitled *An Alan Smithee Film,* with Whoopi Goldberg as the third muscleteer.

2. *Kung Fu Meets the Wild, Wild, West:* Jackie often talks of producing and starring in a movie about cowboys, Indians and Chinese laborers to be filmed in California, and tentatively entitled *The Lion Goes West.* Jackie wants an authentic queue (traditional half-shaved head topped by a long braid)—talk about devotion. **Status:** Who knows? (See "Chan and Abel" sidebar for update.)

3. *Fireman's Story:* Although Jackie had this idea long before *Backdraft,* that movie's release dampened Chan's enthusiastic flame. He never wants to follow. Too bad—a stunt-filled story about firemen would do for the blaze brigade in Hong Kong what *Police Story* did for policemen. **Status:** With the release of the ATV Network TV series *Flame* in Hong Kong as well as a similar series here in the States, the embers are dying.

4. *Smokey II?:* In the late eighties, Jackie mentioned a movie Golden Harvest wanted him to do with Burt Reynolds and Phoebe Cates. In Chan's words, it was supposed to be "another very Americanized film with several international stars." **Status:** Another *Cannonball Run?* Thank goodness the buzz died.

5. *Singapore Sling:* An action comedy to be directed by Richard (*Lethal Weapon*) Donner starring Jackie and either Tom Hanks, Jim Belushi or Randy Quaid. **Status:** It got far enough to have a name. It was quickly put on hiatus—in other words, according to those who have read the premise, happily *forgotten.*

6. *Beverly Hills Ninja:* Suspend your disbelief for a moment and try to imagine an actioner starring Jackie Chan and . . . Chris Farley. Really! People claim to have seen trailers and it was reported in *Variety.* We couldn't make this up. **Status:** Neither could anyone else.

7. **Confucius Brown:** As reported in *Variety* (April 9, 1996), this movie was to star Wesley Snipes and Chan as cousins who battle Chinatown gangsters. Touted as an action-comedy reminiscent of *48 Hours*. **Status:** No word yet. Snipes already had Woody Harrelson as a brother in *Money Train*! Just how big *is* his family?

8. **Pre Karate Kid:** Jackie got the idea to do a story about a young immigrant to the United States who must battle street gangs while he was filming *Battle Creek Brawl*. **Status:** The heads of Golden Harvest said no. And when *Karate Kid* came out, Jackie found that it was close to his original idea. He made *Rumble in the Bronx* instead.

9. **Blood Island:** After *Battle Creek Brawl's* failure, Hal Needham wrote this movie for Jackie as another attempt at American stardom. **Status:** Jackie made his own pirate movie instead, *Project A*—a groundbreaking film for the Hong Kong market.

10. **Jackie's Love Story:** In 1991, Jackie asked his fans their opinion of his making a love story. "I can still remember the complaints we got after my love scene with Kristine De Bell in *Battle Creek Brawl*," he said. **Status:** Although he would love to make a romance that requires little stunt work, response to the idea has been negative.

11. **Green Hornet:** Could you see it? George Clooney and Jackie Chan in a movie based on the Lone Ranger's descendant? What a great Hornet/Kato teaming, but alas, Clooney flew the hive and Jackie never entered. **Status:** "We've been talking about maybe doing the *Green Hornet*," said Jackie in February 1996 to *Video Eyeball*. "I think Golden Harvest is still talking about it. We want to find a big American star maybe, a big actor with me to bring me to the Americans."

12. **Oh Very Nice!:** A rumor appeared in *Apple Daily*, October 3, 1995, concerning a collaboration between Jackie and Chow Yun Fat (*The Killer*). The movie was to be produced by Win's Film Production Company Ltd., Chow's company, and Golden Harvest. **Status:** Jackie's office in Hong Kong made no comment other than to say that nothing is definite and negotiations may or may not be taking place. Chow would only say in his characteristic enigmatic way, "Hmmm . . . me and Jackie together? You think so?"

13. **Dorian Gray:** Just to make a nice baker's dozen: According to *Asian Trash Cinema*, in 1992 Jackie was supposedly on a breakneck schedule, making movies back to back and stockpiling more than twenty-five films. Why? So he can release the films at the rate of two per year while he grows old, his screen image never fading. **Status:** Anyone who knows Jackie's overlong production schedules is laughing themselves silly just . . . about . . . NOW.

wished, not to mention that the story required Jackie to be underwater without an oxygen tank for long periods of time. Conditions while filming at Falls Creek were also harsh. It was impossible to stand on the snow because the cold seeped through the inadequate boots worn by the cast and crew. Shelter took the form of six portable aluminum huts equipped with gas heaters, and lunch was brought down the mountain and transported forty-five minutes in vacuum packs, hardly ever arriving hot. Authenticity has its price. **Bottom line:** This is Jackie's attempt at a James Bond movie. As such, it's not too bad, and the revamped New Line version is better. Don't expect a fight a minute, or you'll be disappointed.

Rating: 👊👊👊

■ NICE GUY
(1997)

Directed by Samo Hung. Starring Jackie Chan and Richard Norton.
Back with big brother Samo, Jackie finished filming *Nice Guy* in Australia for release in 1997.

The premise: A TV cook/celebrity (Chan) becomes privy to some information that the mob wishes he didn't have. Fun and fury ensue.

Film fact: This is Jackie's first sync-sound movie in English. Coproduced with New Line. **Jackie says:** When asked about his choice of directors, Jackie told writer Ricky Miller that Samo "is always the best. Now with Asia, everyone knows that Samo is going down and no one wants to see his movie anymore. It's a very sad thing, so I call him up and we make a movie together again. So, right now, Samo can only direct; he cannot act. Film business is very bad. When you are a success, the film buyer is like, 'Oh, Samo Hung—we want you . . . we need you.' But now, the same buyer tell me, 'Please don't let Samo direct or act in the movie.' It's very difficult. So now, I say, 'No, I want him [Samo] to direct.'" **Rumor has it:** Jackie learned something from filming the

"New York" movie *Rumble in the Bronx* in Vancouver, Canada: "I learned there are no mountains in New York," he told James Brady in *Parade* magazine. "But, everywhere, there is graffiti." So when it came to filming his next "New York" movie, Jackie decided to go elsewhere. "Finally, I said, 'Why not make it Melbourne?'" He didn't know then that the winters in Australia were so cold. "I hate it here," he later said. What's he got against the Big Apple, anyway? **Worst injury:** During the writing of this book, Jackie suffered an injury on the set of *Nice Guy*. **Jackie says:** "I got hurt doing a back somersault," explained Chan in *Parade Magazine*. "Good thing they had a safety box for me. I was out for five or six seconds, and they rushed me to the hospital. My neck got hurt. I couldn't move it. I was like Robocop. But I'm okay now." He promises to take a rest before starting a new film. **Bottom line:** Jackie says he's not too happy with this movie, but that shouldn't dissuade fans from seeing it. He's said the same about *City Hunter* and *Drunken Master II*, and they turned out to be entertaining. Judge for yourself.

Jackie Chan at rest? There ain't no such animal. Already he has been on *The Late Show with David Letterman*, *Late Night with Conan O'Brien*, *The Tonight Show with Jay Leno*, *Fox After Breakfast*, *Good Morning America*, *Prime Time Live*, and *A&E Biography*, and in countless magazines like *GQ*, *TimeOut*, the *New York Times Magazine* and *Vibe* . . . and he's always talking about his next two movies.

■ One of
Jackie's best.
Police Story.

CHANPLOITATION
—OR—
SPECIAL "WHERE NOT TO BUY 'EM" VIDEO REPORT FROM RIC MEYERS

IF "IMITATION IS THE SINCEREST FORM OF FLATTERY," as Charles Caleb Colton said in the nineteenth century, the filmmakers of Asia and knockoff artists of America must be sycophants indeed, since pale plagiarisms of Jackie Chan movies have been perpetrated on two fronts: one, by producers who couldn't think of anything original, and two, by film distributors who slap false names onto credits.

In other words, when buying those Jackie Chan movie tapes for $5.99 at your local video store, beware. You may not be getting what you paid for. Here's why.

Curiously, there was only one attempt to "clone" Jackie Chan, which came after his Hong Kong success in *Drunken Monkey in a Tiger's Eye* (aka *Drunken Master*), when many Hong Kong hack artists started grinding out cheap versions of the same story with titles like *World of the Drunken Master* starring "Jack Long" and *Dance of the Drunken Mantis* starring "Jacky Chen." And since Jackie's international success was thwarted by such lackluster efforts as *The Big Brawl* (aka *Battle Creek*

Ric Meyers is the monthly columnist for *Inside Kung-Fu* magazine and a team member on the *Jackie Chan's Spartan X* comic book (Topps, 1997). His newest novel is *Murder in Halruaa* (TSR Books, 1996).

■ Jackie (l) in *Twinkle, Twinkle, Lucky Stars*.

Brawl), *The Protector* and Chan's contribution to *Cannonball Run*, the rip-offs on this side of the Atlantic were limited to things like *The Jacky Chan Connection*—a rerelease of *To Kill with Intrigue* with a misleading poster that repeatedly proclaimed, "Starring Jacky Chan! Fight Scenes by Jacky Chan! Directed by Jacky Chan!"

But then came *Rumble in the Bronx,* and the true difference between Bruce Lee and Jackie Chan became apparent. For while Bruce is perpetuated with all manner of stand-ins with false names, Jackie is exploited by impostors named, not Jackie Chin, Jackie Chon, or Jackie Chun, but Jackie Chan. The schlock-meisters see no reason to change the name to protect the innocent . . . or guilty.

The problem came with the many movies Jackie made before he became a bona fide star in *Snake in the Eagle's Shadow*. Hong Kong producers thought nothing of selling the video rights to these films to whoever asked for them, and had an unfortunate tendency to go out of business owing money to a variety of creditors—all who claimed rights to the aforementioned films and also thought nothing of repeatedly selling those rights to anybody.

The result is a growing wave of "Chanploitation" that is gripping the video industry. All the films Chan made for Lo Wei have been released by no fewer than four American video distribution companies, including CDDM, Simitar and, best of all, All Seasons Entertainment, who used better-quality tapes, transferred them in SP mode, created the best packaging, and sold their right to *Inside Kung-Fu* magazine.

Of these less than stellar efforts, pick up *Fearless Hyena* and maybe *Half a Loaf of Kung Fu* and *Spiritual Kung Fu*, but give the rest a jaundiced eye. But the Chan-offs don't stop there. A visit to the entertainment stores will reveal a veritable tsunami of strange knockoffs and flat-out fake-outs in the wake of Jackie yanking his video rights back from Tai Seng Video Marketing.

While Chan and company shop for reputable American companies to package his films with the quality that Toho brings to his Japanese tapes, seemingly every rip-off artist on the fringe of martial arts movie fandom is out for the down-and-dirty buck. Ever hear of *Jackie Chan's Bloodpact*, proudly distributed by MNTEX Entertainment? Well, that's because it's actually *Dance of the Drunken Mantis*, one of the many inferior copycat movies made in the wake of *Drunken Master*, which doesn't even feature Jackie (nor does it feature the ninja MNTEX has also put on the video-box art).

How about Jackie Chan in *Ten Fingers of Death*, released by Magnum Video, or *Master with Cracked Fingers*, released by Arena in cooperation with Eastern Heroes? If you've heard of one, you've heard of both,

because they are really the same awful movie—cobbled together by 21st Century Entertainment way back when Jackie was being hyped for *The Big Brawl*. The film itself is a laughable hodgepodge featuring an extremely young Jackie, edited together with an older stuntman who keeps his hand in front of his face. [This film has also been released by Simitar under the name *Eagle Shadow Fist*, boxed with *New Fist of Fury*.—R.W.]

Incredibly, Arena/Eastern Heroes has also released several other

■ A publicity shot for *Police Story III: Supercop*.

Chan come-ons that the buyer should beware, including *Drunken Fist Boxing*, which has cover art stolen from *Drunken Master II*, but is actually another sans-Jackie fraud originally called *The Story of the Drunken Master*. Then there's their *Top Fighter*, an otherwise occasionally commendable documentary that flagrantly steals interviews from the Jackie Chan episode of *The Incredibly Strange Film Show*.

Meanwhile, you might want to miss EDDE Entertainment's subtitled version of *Twin Dragons* that looks like it was videotaped off a Chinatown movie theater screen by some guy in the audience. Even with all these shenanigans, I have to thank Magnum Entertainment for one thing: an amazingly good, subtitled, letterboxed version of *Drunken Master* (which they call *The Drunken Master*) with front and back box art "borrowed" from All Seasons Entertainment's version of *Fearless Hyena*.

Finally, there's Parade Video's *Jackie Chan Rumble Packs*—cleverly conceived, nicely packaged, two-tape knockoffs that take the cake for gall. In what is perhaps an homage to Bruce Lee, the package for the two incredibly cheap SLP-mode tapes for what they call "Round One" (instead of "Volume One") is clearly meant for "Round Two" and vice versa. The homage? Well, the titles for *Fists of Fury* and *The Chinese Connection* were accidentally switched as well when those famous Bruce films came to America.

By any name, these literally tacky tapes (say good-bye to your clean VCR heads!) feature two sad films from Jackie's teenage past as well as a very bad transfer of *Jackie Chan's Police Force*—the dubbed version of *Police Story* that appeared at the New York Film Festival—and *Fists of Chan*, a really terrible "documentary" that is a series of cobbled-together fight scenes from some of Jackie's pre-stardom films . . . as well as from a movie Jackie never even appeared in.

Who knows where the legalities lie on all the aforementioned, but as far as this martial arts movie maniac is concerned, stick with New Line, Miramax, and whichever company the rights for Chan's most recent classics go to. That way the patient kung fu connoisseurs will prosper while the con artists go bust.

■ Jackie does Groucho in *Police Story II*. Yes, that's his real nose!

THE J.C. QUIZ

TEST YOUR KNOWLEDGE of Jackie Chan movies. Now that you've . . . ahem . . . read this whole book, you should know the answers, but just in case, answers do appear below.

■ SECTION ONE:

1. In _____, Jackie is a mute yearning to learn kung fu skills.
2. In _____, Jackie is taught the secret of the five styles by spirits wearing _____.
3. In _____, Jackie's family is killed by a group called the _____ Gang.
4. In _____, Jackie plays one of three men hired to escort a girl and her brother to _____.
5. In *Dragons Forever*, Jackie hits his head on _____.

■ SECTION TWO:

1. Item that Liu Chia Liang loses in *Drunken Master II*?
2. Item that Anita Mui wishes to temporarily sell in *DM II*?
3. In *Operation Condor*, one of the women has a pet _____.
4. In _____, Jackie has a pet squirrel.
5. In *City Hunter*, Jackie thinks that a woman's thigh is actually

   _____.
6. In *Supercop*, May is accused of being what?
7. Movie in which Jackie eats a handful of red peppers?
8. In *Supercop*, actor Bill Tung must disguise himself as

   _____.
9. In *Operation Condor*, Jackie is looking for_____.
10. In *Police Story II*, while looking for a bomb, Jackie retrieves a
    straying _____.
11. In *City Hunter*, Jackie decides that a white _____ would
    make a good lunch.

■ SECTION THREE:

1. In which of the following movies did Jackie not appear in drag?

A. *Young Master*
B. *Project S*
C. *City Hunter*
D. *Fearless Hyena*
E. None of the above

2. In which of the following movies did Jackie not take a shower?

A. *Police Story*
B. *Project A*
C. *Armour of God*

D. *Young Master*

E. None of the above

3. In which of the following movies is Jackie not on the water?

A. *Crime Story*

B. *City Hunter*

C. *Operation Condor*

D. *Project A*

E. None of the above

4. Jackie has not appeared with which of the following comedians?

A. Michael Hui

B. Sammy Davis, Jr.

C. Dean Martin

D. Milton Berle

E. None of the above

5. In which of the following movies is Jackie not in close contact with fire?

A. *Police Story II*

B. *Drunken Master II*

C. *Supercop*

D. *Crime Story*

E. None of the above

■ A tender moment with Maggie Cheung in *Twin Dragons*.

Answers: Section One: (1) *Shaolin Wooden Men*; (2) *Spiritual Kung Fu*, hula shirts; (3) *To Kill With Intrigue*, Killer Bee; (4) *Magnificent Bodyguard*, the Stormy Hills; (5) a ceiling fan. Section Two: (1) jade seal; (2) pearl necklace; (3) scorpion; (4) *Dragonlord*; (5) a chicken wing; (6) a prostitute; (7) *Project A II*; (8) Jackie's mother; (9) a hidden cache of Nazi gold; (10) bouncing ball; (11) rat. Section Three: (1) C.; (2) C.; (3) C.; (4) D.; (5) E.

■ See Jackie jump—*Dragons Forever.*

Author's Afterword

—or—

In a Crystal Ball

Hollywood cinema? Never heard of it. They're all American movies to us. Hong Kong cinema? There *used* to be such a thing. But by the time this book is published, after July 1997, Hong Kong will just be another dot on a rather large map. A dot where perhaps movies are made. *Chinese* cinema.

When the British dropped anchor off the coast of China a hundred years ago, sheltered from typhoons by a nondescript island, they named it the Fragrant Harbor—"Hong Kong." No doubt the smell of bullion they would be able to extract by trading with the inscrutable continent added to the sweetness.

It seems money has always been part of the very air of Hong Kong. From the China traders to the financial bankers to the land speculators to the organized crime triads, and now to the Hong Kong filmmakers.

Since its naming, the still beautiful, rolling island is fronted by a harbor that has become much less fragrant. It's filled with sludge and sunken tankers and is slowly disappearing due to something called reclamation. Soon the watery strip that separates the island from the Kowloon Peninsula will cease to be.

■ Twister, Hong Kong style, in *The Young Master.*

Hong Kong and China will be one. Those of you just discovering the vicarious pleasures of Hong Kong action cinema will thus be saddened to know that, much like the Star Ferry that chugs along a shorter distance every day, you are docking at the end of an era. Not that it hasn't been foreshadowed for many years.

"When I first became a fan of Hong Kong movies," says writer Ric Meyers, "it was phenomenal. You could go to any of the six theaters in New York's Chinatown and see a variety of wonderful movies—every week something different. Now, there is one struggling movie theater left."

Hong Kong movies have been their own worst enemies. For every Jackie Chan, who has unlimited budgets and time, there are many other actors and actresses who churn out four or five movies a year of dubious quality. For every actress that becomes a respected regular, there are many who are beaten or raped by triads trying to run the lucrative industry much as they would a drug cartel or a prostitution ring.

"When a theater in Chinatown started showing porno movies, we knew it was not long for this world," says Meyers. "It would close down within a year."

Not to blame the triads entirely, the pirating of Hong Kong movies has also led to the industry's downfall. Just like a drug dealer who eventually kills off his own buyers, bootleggers cut into the gross of area theaters, causing cinemas to close down and ultimately decreasing the demand for movies, leading to cessation of good movies being made.

"You can put a policeman in each theater to catch them," says Jackie. "But even then, you don't know in which theater the illegal copy is made."

For years, Jackie's movies (along with the occasional Stephen Chow, Jet Li, or Andy Lau flick) were the only films that kept the Chinatown theaters open in the United States, despite the fact that you could buy bootleg copies down the street from said theaters weeks before a movie opened. The pickin's have been slim. No wonder Chan is cultivating new markets like the United States—even China.

While others are scared of what China's takeover of Hong Kong in 1997 will bring, Jackie is getting his foothold, filming in the once-forbidden country, and becoming the first Hong Kong director/actor whose movies appear there on the big screen, not just on illegal video copies. For Jackie, the reason for his acceptance into this world power, known for its strict, blackballing film codes, is clear.

"All these years, there is no politics in my movies and also I don't like politics. If you want to release in China, you have to cooperate with the Chinese government then you can release in China. Big market," explains Chan. "At times, my movies would not cooperate with China, I film in some other country, but they still let it be released in China."

Nevertheless, time is running out, and the roller-coaster ride is moving into the station. Unlike the famous Cyclone coaster of Coney Island, the attendant won't let you keep your seat for two dollars more and go on the exciting, thrilling, adrenaline-pumping ride again. It will be reshaped. Maybe it will become a Ferris wheel, or a whirligig . . . or maybe one of those rides that spins around and the floor . . . drops out.

If we had a crystal ball, perhaps we could look toward the future. But could any orb capture the unpredictability of a Communist government? Instead, we must wait . . . much like the Hong Kong people themselves . . . and see.

Jackie Chan, in this situation *is*, essentially, the King of Siam (read that: Hong Kong), with responsibilities not only to himself but to his country and his subjects (read that: audience). Like that character of life, literature, celluloid, and lore, Jackie is headstrong, stubborn, acceptance-seeking and proud. He is also gentle, endearing, kind and hungry for knowledge. Whereas the king grasps for the right path in a country facing great change, Jackie looks for his path in his own changing city while facing the inevitable limitations of age coupled with the possibility of a new frontier. Like Yul Brynner in his performance as the famous king (they were both bald at one time too!), the right path must mean the path of dignity—the path with the most "face" (read: respect).

"I'll stay in Hong Kong," says Jackie. "If 1997 comes and the China government says 'Jackie, you cannot make this kind of movie anymore and you cannot live in this town,' either I will die or I'll just quit. But I do not think they'll do that. As long as I'm making Jackie Chan movies, I'll be okay."

Despite this optimistic hope, as Chan becomes more of a recognizable figure in America, perhaps he will be spending less time in Hong Kong out of sheer necessity. The William Morris Agency, which now represents him in his stateside endeavors, wants him to make two movies in 1997 alone. As Hong Kong loses its freedom, Jackie Chan is more free than ever before. What does he have to prove? Nothing. Stunts and movies for him have been a piece of cake for twenty years.

"My father tells me, 'So, I'm sixty-five and I can still cook—what about you?'" Jackie humorously reported to *Combat* magazine in 1992. "I say, 'Yeh, yeh, yeh . . .'"

As long as Jackie Chan can still be involved in making movies. . . . Somewhere, he'll always be *dying for action.*

CATCHING UP WITH JACKIE

ROUND TABLE INTERVIEW: July 23, 1996, New York City. Ric Meyers from *Inside Kung-Fu* magazine, along with freelance writers Renée Witterstaetter, Alex Jay, and other members of the New York press.

Press: Jackie, what is your next movie?

Jackie: Because I hurt my neck [making *Nice Guy*], I thought about a new story. A very good story—*Police Story V.* As soon as I hurt my neck I went to the hospital for X rays. It takes two hours. Suddenly I got an idea. At the beginning of *Police Story V,* I'll go to buy a ring. This time Maggie's family says, "You sure you want to marry Jackie?" I have some mission to do—a big case. Couple of police get injured. I get injured. Go to hospital. I get hurt on the head—unconscious. Flashback to *Police Story.* See! Good, hah! I have a big stunt, then flashback to *Police Story II, III, IV.* When finished with all these, I look for my girlfriend. Call home, nobody is there. Suddenly I learn that Maggie is paralyzed. But maybe that's too sad. Maybe a broken leg. But she cannot walk, cannot talk. Day before yesterday I called up Stanley Tong. I told him the story. He almost cried, because I have a very good drama in the middle. Flash

to Maggie learning how to walk. How to say things. At the end, I won't tell you what happens. This will be the first movie without outtakes. No more outtakes. Outtakes we'll put in *The Making of Police Story V.* Really exciting! I always try to think of new stories because they interest me . . . now because I hurt my neck.

Renée: Will you film in Hong Kong?
Jackie: No, no more Hong Kong. Hong Kong cannot make a Jackie Chan movie anymore. Too small.

Renée: China?
Jackie: Yeah, China's okay. China's big. Hong Kong is such a small town. All the noise. All these years, I've been filming everywhere in Hong Kong. Everybody knows [the locations]! And also it's very difficult to shoot. Hong Kong people don't cooperate with the film people. "Go away!" They won't go away. They just stand there. When we film some other place—even in China—we're glad when we shoot there because people don't bother us. You were there!

Renée: Except the army guys. They wouldn't leave.
Jackie: The army guys! Every day I go out, I have my bodyguard with me—weighs 220 or something. But on the set there are a hundred [soldiers].

Renée: I thought they were going to kill us that one day when they pressed against the van.
Jackie: You know how many people were on that mountain? They weren't going to eat! They were just going to stand there all day and watch me!

Ric: So, are you finished filming *Nice Guy*?
Jackie: Seven more days. I know American market is very important,

so I stopped *Nice Guy* and came here to promote *Supercop*. I still think I need more time to let the American audience know me. So, I stop. My boss, Raymond [Chow] is very angry. Because we stopped—seven days—is three and a half million Hong Kong dollars. If I didn't come here, we'd be finished by now. I don't care—I just bought the ticket and came. It's most important, for us, for future. It was a very good beginning—*Rumble in the Bronx* in February. Seems everybody liked it. So, I hope to do the promotion now and then go back [to Australia to finish film]. If it [*Supercop*] doesn't do any good, I'm satisfied, because I've come already. I came—did the promotion—still not good, okay. That means I did my best, American audiences didn't like it coming out. If I'm not here and the movie does badly, then I blame myself. This is why I have to come.

Press: Have you committed to any films in Hollywood?
Jackie: No.

Press: Nothing?
Jackie: *Too* many projects. Just *too* many projects. I've been talking here, talking there. Some company, they just want me, "Ah, you're new boy!" "Now you're hot—I want you." I say, "You want me—twenty-two million." "What!" "Stallone gets twenty million." "Yeah." "Your movie, give me twenty-two million." Or I work for Steven Spielberg for free. Or give me a good project, good script, good director, good leading actress, leading actor, then you have a good movie. Okay! One half million, I'll do it. So, I'm very careful coming into America—either I make my own movies or I have to know the director, I have to know the script. I have many scripts in my mind.

Alex: What about John Woo? You worked with him years ago?
Jackie: Yeah, his first movie.

Alex: Would you like to work with him again?

Jackie: I think . . . yes. Yes. I guess, yes. I think . . . I'd be better off to find some other director first. Because I already know John Woo. I know his style. For me . . . maybe for America audience, me with John Woo, "Ah, work with John Woo, ah, good!" For me, it's nothing exciting. I would rather work with somebody else.

Press: Who? Which director?

Jackie: Oh, there are too many.

Press: Name one.

Jackie: First choice—like Steven. Also I think James Cameron. Because I want to learn blue screens. So this way if I can use half blue screen and half computer, I don't have to jump from ten stories to the helicopter. But I'll still jump—maybe twenty feet. Then with the blue screen, there's more safety. No good, we can do it again.

Alex: Do you think you were crazy for doing the jump in *Supercop*?

Jackie: No, I'm *so* happy I did it! That was four years ago. If we did it right now, I wouldn't jump.

Alex: No?

Jackie: Yeah! Oh, maybe when the time came, I'd jump. But when it looks like some other stunt—no. Like in *Police Story*, jump from the chandelier—I'm so happy I did it. Right now, I wouldn't do it. I'm not going to do it.

Press: So, you haven't done a stunt of that magnitude since then?

Jackie: Stunt for me—every movie I have to find a new stunt. So I think at a certain age, I'm thinking about certain stunts. Even at this age—now forty-two—I wouldn't think of jumping from the same chandelier. Right? I think of something else. Ten years ago, I said, "Yeah, chandelier!" "Jump helicopter!" You know, different time. It's different now.

Ric: Is fighting becoming old to Hong Kong audiences?

Jackie: I think I would bring back more. Asian audiences support me. That's why all Hong Kong movies are going down, except my movies are still at the top. One year—one movie. Always big production. Like *Supercop*—it may be a small production by American standards, like a B movie. Only cost fifteen million Hong Kong dollars. American TV show cost twenty million Hong Kong dollars. I think they're use to these budgets in Asia, and they still like it. But for America, this is new. Some of you guys know me. Okay, you know what I'm doing. But some young kids, young people, just out to see *Rumble in the Bronx*, say, "Ah, new actor! Very good!" I'm not new. I'm antique! I'm the Asian antique. Everybody knows I've been doing these kind of things many, many years.

Press: Have you ever thought about doing a movie with your number one fan Quentin Tarantino?

Jackie: I just had dinner with him a couple of days ago. He had some good ideas, but I don't know if it works or not. I don't know. Then I said, "Okay, you go ahead. Write a script first." Then I see how the script comes out.

Press: Does he want you to star, or will it be an ensemble?

Jackie: Star. Yeah . . . he always thinking about some crazy things.

Press: Do you have a project with Ang Lee?

Jackie: We did talk. But I find out in America that when you talk, you wait five years.

Ric: Maybe seven years!

Jackie: Because Ang Lee, he's very . . . he has lots of pressure. Ang

Lee—especially Ang Lee. I think, he's the kind of director that takes time. Slowly. Slowly. Not like me. I think about a script. Yes! Do it! Like *Police Story V*, I came to Hong Kong this month, I started it. I just start. I have a hospital scene—I started the hospital scene first. As soon as I started the hospital thing, I think, "What is the mission?" You know, I can do that. But the Americans, no, they have to have script first. I have another script in South Africa. Very good! Ah! That's a script! I want to direct myself now.

Ric: Oh, good!
Jackie: Yeah!

Ric: Do you want to direct more in the future?
Jackie: You know what the problem is, when I direct myself, I have the full responsibility. I know everything to be done. Right now, I hire a certain director to direct me. But some other directors I have fired, as you know. Fire. Change. Fire. Change. Even someone like Stanley Tong, if I'm not on set I don't like it. Maybe he's satisfied. You're satisfied. But for my part, I'm not satisfied. I think it's too violent. But he thinks, "Ah, I left violence out already." But when I shoot, you can see a Jackie Chan movie. Even when I'm not directing, you will see a certain style. I'm more human. I have more comedy. I am more reasonable. Like in *Rumble in the Bronx* someone put a gun on me when acting, I'm scared. I'm this kind of person. Sometimes when I'm not on the set, I come back and see some directors, I look at what they are doing, and I'm not satisfied. They're not ready. I finish the scene.

Alex: You don't want graphic violence?
Jackie: I hate violence. I have a lot of comedy. Because all that fighting, machine guns, explosions when it continues for ten minutes, you'll find out it's too much. But if I drop something in the middle, something funny, it's better. You forget. You're still smiling. So, comedy is very important. Too many children see my movies. I hate violence.

Renée: Were you offered the lead in *Farewell My Concubine?*

Jackie: Yes. When they first came to me, I said yes. I wanted to change my . . . I don't want to always be fighting, fighting, fighting. Sometime, somehow, I want to change. When I wanted to do *Crime Story*, I wanted to change. Different kind of police. Then suddenly I wanted to do *City Hunter*. I wanted to do more comedy. I want to try a lot of different things.

Renée: Was the story in *Farewell My Concubine* very much like your own childhood?

Jackie: Yeah, yeah. The studio did not want me to do it.

Renée: Closer than *Painted Faces?*

Jackie: Hmmm . . . yes. *Painted Faces* was not even twenty percent.

Ric: Is *First Strike* out next?

Jackie: Yes. *First Strike*, then *Operation Condor*. You know what? I'm very happy. I made New Line and Miramax become good friends. I make them sit together to talk. Because New Line has certain pictures and Miramax has certain pictures. If they released at the same time, I'd be finished. So this is why we have the deal now—every six months release a Jackie Chan movie. So now on the *Rumble in the Bronx* tape, they have a *Supercop* trailer. On the *Supercop* tape they have a *First Strike* trailer. January—*First Strike*. August—*Operation Condor*. January—*Nice Guy*. August—*Drunken Master II*. Because I need time. Right now if you put out *Drunken Master II*—some of you who know me will go, "Yes, Jackie Chan." Some other new person after five minutes might walk away. If they know me, they will sit down. So this is why I let them have confidence as to what kind of movie I make, then I put out the period movie.

Ric: I read an interview that said you would retire in three or four years. You don't sound like a man who is retiring.

Jackie: Yes, I just love movies.

Renée: How will 1997 affect you?

Jackie: Nothing, really. A lot of directors and actors immigrated already. America. Canada. They are gone already. Except me. I still hold a Hong Kong passport. I have full confidence. They won't do anything to me. First there is the image. If Jackie Chan goes away . . . ahhh . . . a lot of people go away. And also I'm not political. Even if the Chinese government interviews me, I'll say I don't like Communists. But I know I'm Chinese. I love China. But I don't like politics. I'm just a filmmaker. I just make my films. But in my films there are no politics. It's okay.

Alex: Was *Supercop* the first you filmed in China?

Jackie: First time. Second time *Drunken Master II*.

Renée: Was it difficult to film in China?

Jackie: For me, I think so because it's me, no. Wherever I go, there are bodyguards. It's very safe for me. Whatever I want: "I want that." "Yes." "I want that." "Yes."

Press: Did you use the people in China on the movie?

Jackie: No. Jackie Chan people. Everywhere I go I bring my own people. That's very important. In the U.S. I will bring my own team to sit beside me, to learn, to watch. Really. But definitely I will bring my own stuntmen because it's different. I need the people who can fight with me. I really hope to learn new things like blue screens and special effects.

Renée: On an American film, will you have control?

Jackie: Ah, it's a dilemma. If I want total control I cannot make any movies in America. I will have to go back to Asia. But, on the other hand, if I continue to do this kind of Jackie Chan movie, I will never learn American movies. So this is why I want to come, at least do one or two. To learn. It depends on if it's the right time or not.

Press: How was your experience on *The Protector*?

Jackie: Because I have this kind of experience, it makes me go back to Asia to make my own films. Because of *The Protector*. The director never listened to me. That made me very angry. Then I made *Police Story* for you. In Hollywood, they have bad directors and good directors. Like John Woo, when he came, it's not a John Woo movie anymore, it's a special effect movie—*Broken Arrow*.

Renée: *Hard Target* was cut a lot, later.

Jackie: Yeah, Jean-Claude cut it. Now I also have that script in South Africa.

Renée: And the next *Police Story* movie?

Jackie: That one I'm still thinking about, because I don't have the middle. What mission I'll be doing. What big stunt I'll be doing. I need to think of something to match the good story.

Renée: And the South Africa movie?

Jackie: The South Africa movie is also good. South Africa is more dramatic. The first shot, when I open my eyes, I'm in the middle of nowhere. Around me are the natives. They save me. What I'm wearing is very modern. I've been hurt, but I recover. You now what the title is? *Who Am I?* I don't know who I am. No memory. How did I come to be in the middle of nowhere? And when I talk to the natives, they don't know. I get very angry. "Who am I?" Then all the natives call me "Who Am I." Somehow I get back to the city and find my hotel and my room. All my clothes and a passport—I find out who I am. Who am I? Then I find a British passport, Japanese passport, Spanish passport. There's too many passports. All my pictures! Different names. I still don't know who I am. Then I find out I have no fingerprints. Very dramatic. People chase after me. At the end, very funny. I keep the secret. I always think of my own script.

Press: Which of your films is your favorite?
Jackie: Right now, none. I think the next one.

Press: Oh, come on.
Jackie: Okay, if you are talking about really liking it, I think *Police Story.*

Press: Was the American version of *Supercop* cut down?
Jackie: Yes, I cut it down a little bit because I didn't like it.

Renée: And the music was changed?
Jackie: Oh, ten times better than the Asian version.

Ric: You think so?
Jackie: Yes, yes.

Ric: How about the dubbing?
Jackie: All the things in English I don't like, but the music brings color. Dolby system. Ah!

Press: Will movies still be made in Hong Kong?
Jackie: They're still there. But right now, seven days—one movie. They make just very local movies. Whenever the news comes out—"Man Rapes 11 Girls"—somebody, Wong Jing, already releases a movie: *Man Rapes 11 Girls.* Gets fast money in seven days, cheating the public. In Hong Kong, all movies are going down. Top Ten are all American movies—never happened before. Now everything is American movies.

Renée: Is there a lot of crime in the Hong Kong movie business?
Jackie: NO MORE! They're all gone.

■ Jackie and his longtime manager, Willie Chan.

Press: Which American actress or actor would you like to work with?
Jackie: Oh, I like them . . . it doesn't mean I want to work with them.
I like Jodie Foster, Barbra Streisand. Good talents. They know how to act.
They know how to direct. I like people that know how to direct. Being a
director, you must have talent. Like Jodie Foster—she does everything.
But I don't want to work with some actresses. I want to find new talent.
If I work with Jodie Foster, I think there would be a lot of trouble.

Renée: Robert De Niro?
Jackie: Oh, my all-time hero. Like Muhammad Ali. Oh, I cried when I
saw him at the Olympics.

■ A little off the top in *Dragons Forever.*

WEB SITES

GET WIRED WITH JACKIE
—WEB SITE REVIEWS BY MICHAEL
MIKAELIAN

IF YOU'VE BEEN A FAN OF CHAN FOR A WHILE, you've probably searched high and low for newspaper articles, video clips and magazine interviews pertaining to your favorite Hong Kong movie star, director, stuntman and singer. Depending on your reading habits, you may have seen the interview with Jackie in *Black Belt*, *Axcess*, *M.A.M.A* or *Entertainment Weekly*. If you've been surfing the Internet in search of such things, you'd have little trouble finding them. If you check out the World Wide Web sites below, you'll have even less.

■ JACKIE CHAN'S OFFICIAL WEB SITE:
First stop on the infotainment superhighway!

Where: http://www.jackiechan.com/
Who: Who else? The man himself!
Why: With the amount of activity being generated by his fans, it only makes sense. Without an "official" Jackie Chan Web site, who can you trust, really?
Why should I care: It's official! Anything that you read here can be considered to have come straight from Jackie. Take his heartfelt introduction:

Hello! It is nice to see you in my home page. How are you doing! [Yes, this is my official home page.] Just want to let you know I'm so happy to meet you here. Through this home page, I have confidence that we will communicate better than ever. It doesn't matter where you are now. Just let me know how you feel, and what you want to share with me. This home page is still under construction, I am sure you will give me your thoughts on my home page. Anyway, there will be more information about myself very soon. At the moment, you can follow the links to My Photos Gallery, Filmography and Achievement. Otherwise, you can take a look at my mega movie, *Thunderbolt*.

Like the man says, you can find photos, a filmography and a complete list of his film credits and awards. With time and feedback, this site will probably improve in leaps and bounds (much like Jackie), possibly to become the best Chan Web site. It only seems appropriate that it should.

Next we'll take a look at a few of the sites which I feel really capture the essence of what a Jackie Chan Web site is all about.

■ ANOTHER JACKIE CHAN PAGE, KIDDIES:
New page that is still growing.

Where: www.lava.net/~headrush/jc.html
Who: By a Chan fan, of course.
Why: This is an overall resource page, offering a plethora of things useful and amusing to Chan fans.
Why should I care: News flashes, general bio info, a list of injuries, various magazine articles, photos, filmography and much more are included.

■ CHAN FESTIVAL

Where: //www.filmzone.com/Chan
Why: To celebrate the spirit that is Chan with a staggering multimedia blitz.

Who: The Chanimaniacs at FilmZone, creator's of New Line's Rumble page.
Why should I care: It's a great place for new JC fans, as it covers his major works with summaries, photos and video clips. Vivid graphics keep it interesting for the experienced fan.

■ THE WILD AND CRAZY STUNTMAN/ACTION STAR/MARTIAL ARTIST JACKIE CHAN

Where: http://www.lava.net/~headrush/jc
Who: HeadRush, a Hong Kong movie enthusiast, fan of the perfect wave and all things Hawaiian.
Why: Because it makes him feel good to see it done right.
Why should I care: HeadRush has described Jackie Chan better than any of his contemporaries—as the wild and crazy stuntman/action star/martial artist. I'll admit that his site was the first one I logged on to, but I was impressed with what I saw. After looking at all the others (some more graphically appealing), this one stood out. He had "Who?," "Filmography," "Black-N-Blue Articles," "His Top 10," "HeadRush's Choices," "Links" and "Updates." "Who?" is a well-developed two-part text about Jackie Chan's background. It was so long, it needed two pages! "His Top Ten" is a list of Jackie Chan's ten most favorite movies of all time. I won't spoil it for you, but there was at least one *Godfather* movie on the list . . . "Black-N-Blue Articles" provides links to various articles posted elsewhere on-line. "Links" also provided links, but to other Web sites that might interest a Chan fan. "HeadRush's Choices" showcases the author's favorite Chan flicks. "Updates" features the latest additions for regular readers. (Now, that's what I call service!)

■ JACKIE CHAN FAN

Where: http://www.ee.fit.edu/users/bergman/chan.html
Who: Mr. Bergman.

Why: Because Bergman's a fan.

Why should I care: Although this wasn't the most thorough site (it's not like these guys get paid to do this! Sheesh!), it does have a library of down-loadable images. Also, the filmography here has a really cool little picture of the movie poster next to the bulleted summary (very professional). For a quick Jackie fix, this site is it!

■ THE TEMPLE OF JACKIE CHAN

Where: http://www.pitt.edu/~oren/jackie.html
Who: Oren.
Why: Too much free time. . . .
Why should I care: The Temple of Jackie Chan represents the ultimate expression of fan appreciation, and it's a nice site too. Graphically, this site is very compelling. The layout and design are some of the best I've seen in this search. The site is fun to look at and contains a good deal of information. Overall, it's very entertaining. If you believe in both image and substance, this may very well be your favorite Jackie Chan Web site.

■ Making incense offering in *Dragon Lord.*

■ PROJECT A: AN UNOFFICIAL JACKIE CHAN WEB SITE

Where: http://www.ssc.com/~gary/chan.html
Who: Gary, with a little help from several contributors.
Why: More than a Web site; like a literary compilation.
Why should I care: Gary is humble in his approach to assembling this Web page. Like before, we now have a group of fans who are willing to give much of their time to what some may only ever see as a hobby. While scanning this site, I felt like I was in the Jackie Chan clubhouse, and these guys

were presenting the monthly newsletter. According to Gary, he's always looking for contributions to the site. Who knows? Maybe you'll find your name next to a piece of juicy Jackie gossip one day on the Project A site.

Some other sites of interest include:

■ "JACKIE CHAN!"

(http://brain.isdn.uiuc.edu/~Gen13/jacky.html and http://www.walrus.com/~mindbomb/jackie.html).

These two sites are very similar. If I said any more, I'd be giving the whole thing away.

The following sites are not so much Chan Web sites as they are individual pages that are part of a larger collection. Still, they are quite entertaining.

■ JACKIE CHAN MOVIE REVIEW

Where: http://www.cs.nmsu.edu/~wdawes/Jackie.html
Who: Dawes goes deeply into the plot of each movie, and gives his personal impressions of each one. Reading this is like having a long, intelligent discussion with another fan.
Why should I care: For those of you who like to take your time and read in-depth critical analysis, this site may be of some interest. It's completely dedicated to movies in that Jackie not only stars but also directs.

■ THE JACKIE CHAN STUNTOGRAPHY

Where: http://www.hotwired.com/renfeatures/96/13/stuntography.html
Why should I care: This page has a great collection of actual movie clips that can be downloaded and viewed on your PC!

■ JACKIE CHAN—THE BIG LIST O'STUNTS

Where: http://www.sscnet.ucla.edu/ssc/consult/duong/jackie/
Why should I care: What we have here is a chart cross-referencing each Jackie Chan movie with injuries he suffered during production. Painfully entertaining!

■ JACKIE CHAN INTERVIEW

Where: http://www.eagle.american.edu/eagle/v70/i26/features/chan.ra.html
Why should I care: What you get when you log on to this page is an actual recording of an interview with Jackie Chan in New York. Of course, you have to download it, and you need RealAudio to listen to it. Just think, now your computer can quote Jackie Chan!

■ ROCK RECORDS

Where: http://zero.com.hk/rock/rock2.html
Why should I care: Graphically, this site is top-notch. Rock Records, producer of many Hong Kong rock albums, has a selection of Jackie Chan CDs. Keep up to date on all the latest releases.

■ HONG KONG MOVIE LINKS

Where: http://casa.colorado.edu/~kachun/hkdenver.html
Why should I care: This site will prove invaluable in locating all sorts of other Web pages pertaining to Hong Kong movies. This page is loaded (and I mean loaded) with links to other sites. You have to see it to believe it!

■ TOTALLY UNOFFICIAL JACKIE CHAN PAGE

Where: http://home.gvi.net/~death/chan.html
Why should I care: If all you're interested in is downloading oodles of cool Jackie Chan photos, this is *the* place to do it. Just make sure you have a book nearby and can afford ten to fifteen minutes of Net time to load the entire page. This is the single largest page I've ever seen (over 120,000 bytes!) and it's completely dedicated to pictures! The only thing I should warn you about is . . . all of these pictures come from other Web sites. This means that as of this writing, almost every picture available anywhere else should be available here. Just don't expect to find something here that's nowhere else.

■ RUMBLE IN THE BRONX PREVIEW PAGE

Where: http://www.ios.com/~sahpngyi/contents.html
Why should I care: For an unofficial site, this stuff is good! On these pages, you can download photos from the film, Quicktime movies, and behind-the-scenes shots. Be sure to check it out!

■ JACKIE CHAN: THE BUSTER KEATON OF ASIA

Where: http://www.ids.net/~picpal/jchan.html
Why should I care: Looking for that hard-to-find film? Picture Palace offers a long list of Jackie Chan movies, and you can follow the links to other pages to find out how to order. Overall, Picture Palace offers a selection of fifty thousand movies!

Besides Web sites, you can also check out the Asian Movies alternate newsgroup (another entirely different thing you can do with your modem).

■ Scaling new heights in *Project A*.

CHAN ACHIEVEMENTS

Year	Title	Organization	Territory
1983	Best Actor	*RoadShow* magazine	Japan/Worldwide
1984	Best Actor, Foreign	*RoadShow* magazine	Japan/Worldwide
1985	Best Actor, Foreign	*RoadShow* magazine	Japan/Worldwide
1986	Jackie Chan Day (9-6-86)	San Francisco	United States
1986	Ten Outstanding Young Persons of Hong Kong	Hong Kong Junior Chamber of Commerce	Hong Kong
1986	Best Actor	*RoadShow* magazine	Japan/Worldwide
1987	Best Actor	*RoadShow* magazine	Japan/Worldwide
1988	Best Actor/Director	*RoadShow* magazine	Japan/Worldwide
1988	Outstanding Young Persons of the World	Jaycees International	Japan/Worldwide
1989	Member of the Most Excellent Order of the British Empire	British government	Hong Kong

Year	Title	Organization	Territory
1989	Best Actor	Artists' Guild	Hong Kong
1990	Des Insignes de Chevalier des Arts et des Lettres	The Cinémathèque Française	France/Worldwide
1992	The Five Most Outstanding Young Chinese of the World	Taiwan government	Taiwan/Worldwide
1992	Ten Most Healthy Personalities of Hong Kong	Radio & Television	Hong Kong
1992	Best Actor	Golden Horse Award	Taiwan
1993	Outstanding Contribution to Movie Award	Asia Pacific Film Festival	Asia/Pacific
1993	Best Actor	Golden Horse	Taiwan
1994	Best Actor	Cine-Asia	Worldwide
1995	Lifetime Achievement Award	MTV	Worldwide
1995	Honorary Vice President of the Girl Guides Association	The Hong Kong Girl Guides Association	Hong Kong
1995	The Hong Kong Tourism Ambassador	The Hong Kong Tourist Association	Hong Kong
1995	Honorable Doctorate	The Baptist University	Hong Kong
1996	Jackie Chan Day (3-6-96)	Illinois state government	Illinois
1996	Jackie Chan Day	Chicago city government	Chicago

■ ORGANIZATIONS:

1987–present
>Jackie Chan Charitable Foundation—Hong Kong, Founder.

1988–present
>Jackie Chan Charitable Foundation—Japan, Founder.

1989–1991
>Hong Kong Director Guild Executive Committee, Member

1991–1993
>Hong Kong Director Guild, Vice-President

1993–present
>Hong Kong Director Guild, President

1992–present
>Hong Kong Stuntmen Association, Member

1993–present
>Hong Kong Society of Cinematographers, Honorary President

1993–present
>Hong Kong Performance Artiste Guild, Vice-President

1994–present
>Motion Picture Association, Hong Kong, President

■ *Police Story III: Supercop.*

■ The long leg of the law—*Police Story.*

THE JACKIE CHAN NETWORK

WANT TO KNOW MORE ABOUT JACKIE CHAN? Here are a few addresses to help you get started.

■ FAN CLUBS:

Jackie Chan Fan Club, USA
Joy Al-Sofi
P.O. Box 2281
Portland, OR 97208

Jackie Chan Fan Club International
Davis Fung
145 Waterloo Rd.
Kowloon, Hong Kong

Jackie Chan Fan Club UK
Richard Cooper
P.O. Box 1989
Bath
BA2 2YE
United Kingdom

Jackie Chan Fan Club Australia
Christine Mullen
P.O. Box 795
Gladesville
New South Wales 2111
Australia

Jackie Chan Fan Club Japan
Tadashi Iida
26 Banchi
Sakamachi
Shinujuku-ku
Tokyo 160
Japan

Canadian Jackie Chan Fan Club
Stephanie Presando
3007 Kingston Rd.
Box 109
Scarborough
Ontario, Canada

■ MAGAZINES:

Eastern Heroes
96 Shaftsbury Ave.
London, W1V 7DH
England

Hong Kong Film Connection
P.O. Box 867225
Plano, TX 75086-7225

Hong Kong Film Magazine
601 Van Ness Avenue
Suite E3728
San Francisco, CA 94102

Impact
M.A.I. Publications
Revenue Chambers
St. Peter's Street
Huddersfield
HD1 1DL
England

M.A.M.A (Martial Arts Movie Associates)
William Connolly
6635 Delongpre #4
Hollywood, CA 90028

Inside Kung Fu
CFW Enterprises
4201 Vanowen Pl.
Burbank, CA 91505

Topps Comics
One Whitehall St.
New York, NY 10004

■ FILM COMPANIES, FILM DISTRIBUTORS AND VIDEO SALES:

Golden Harvest
8 King Tung St.
Hammer Hill Rd.
Kowloon, Hong Kong

Miramax
375 Greenwich St.
New York, NY 10013

New Line Cinema
116 N. Robertson Blvd.,
Suite 200
Los Angeles, CA 90048

Rim Film Distributors, Inc.
9884 Santa Monica Blvd.
Beverly Hills, CA 90212

Tai Seng, Video Marketing, Inc.
170 South Spruce Ave.,
Suite 200
South San Francisco, CA
94080
(Copyright holder of many
Chan films)

World Video & Supply, Inc.
150 Executive Park Blvd., Suite
1200
San Francisco, CA 94134
(Carries two Chan movies)

Simitar Entertainment, Inc.
3850 Annapolis Lane, Suite
140
Plymouth, MN 55447
(Most of the Lo Wei movies
can be obtained from this company. Ask for SP mode only.)

■ RETAIL OUTLETS:

Advantage Video
P.O. Box 5224
Willowick, OH 44095

Asia Television Video (ATV)
328 S.E. 82nd Ave.
Portland, OR 97216

Dragon Art
P.O. Box 9307
N. Hollywood, CA 91609
(Movie related material)

Pix Poster Cellar
1105 Mass Ave. #10
Cambridge, MA 02138

Stage & Screen
2410 McKinney
Dallas, TX
(Movie related material)

Ztarz Catalogue
412-416 World Commerce
Center
11 Canton Rd.
Kowloon, Hong Kong
(Hong Kong movie collectibles)

GLOSSARY

STOP! Important things in the all-encompassing world of Jackie Chan and his movies:

Air: Jackie is familiar with this element, as he flies through it often—to a hot air balloon, to a helicopter rope ladder, to the roof of a bus, etc.

Ali, Muhammad: Boxer Jackie admires most.

Anchors Away: Movie most likely to have inspired performance in *Spiritual Kung Fu.*

Andrews, Julie: American songstress. One of Chan's favorites.

Asian Hawk: Jackie's name in *Armour of God.*

Astaire, Fred: Chan model for grace and agility.

Barker, Bob: Game show host who once trained with Jackie before Chan became a star. Oddly, Barker is slugged by Adam Sandler in *Happy Gilmore,* and Sandler goes on to beat out Chan for the MTV Best Fight Award in 1995 for that scene. Small world.

Birthday: Just another twenty-four hour period for Jackie.

Bloody Palm: Technique used to kill a diplomat in *Spiritual Kung Fu.*

Bo Bo Chah: Tea bearing Jackie's name.

Bow to the King: One of three fake styles in *Half a Loaf of Kung Fu.*

"Can't Help Falling in Love": Jackie's favorite Elvis song. He recently gave his version on the TV shows *Fox After Breakfast* and *Conan O'Brien.*

Capra, Frank: Harold Lloyd's former gagman. Directed films such as the perennial *It's a Wonderful Life.* Chan discovered through Capra a kindred sympathy for the common man.

CH 28: Jackie's license plate. That's his own car in *Twin Dragons.*

Chan, Kevin: Jackie's name in *Police Story.*

Chan, Willie: Manager. (See "Chan Squared" sidebar.)

Chan's Folly: Willie's name for The Macau Grand

Prix and the Hong Kong one million that Jackie spends to enter.

Chaplin, Charlie: Silent comedian. Chan influence.

Cha Shu Bow: Favorite breakfast food—steamed pork buns.

Cheung, Maggie: Hong Kong actress cast as Chan's girlfriend in *Police Story*.

China Drama Academy: Peking Opera school Jackie attended from ages seven through seventeen.

Chinese Artifacts: What foreigners are always stealing in Hong Kong patriotic dramas.

Chinese New Year: Holiday in February—big movie release date.

Ching Wu School: Meaning "Unity and Resistance." A school set up to fight Japanese occupation during World War II in *New Fist of Fury*.

Chocolate Cake: One of the two things Jackie could order on his first visit to America before learning English.

Chow, Raymond: Head of Golden Harvest.

City Hunter: Popular Japanese comic book. Inspired Chan's movie of the same name.

Coffee: One of the two things that Jackie could order on his first visit to America before learning English.

Colt/Jackie Chan Trophy: Racing trophy at the Macau Grand Prix.

Concubine: One of three fake styles in *Half a Loaf of Kung Fu*.

Crane: One of the five animal styles of martial arts. Direct with purpose.

Crazy Bull: Troublemaker in *Twin Dragons*.

Crazy Horse: Dynamite salesman at the Neptune Bar in *Police Story II*.

Daniels, Gary: English martial artist who spars with Jackie in *City Hunter*. Remembered for his well-executed splits and his portrayal of Ken from the *Mortal Kombat* video game parody.

Dragon: One of the five animal styles of martial arts. Representing agility in the mind.

Dragon Ma: Jackie's name in the *Project A* series.

Earth: Jackie has had some unhappy run-ins with this element—namely when he comes face-to-face . . . er, head to rock . . . with it in *Armour of God*. In *Rumble in the Bronx*, thanks to the hovercraft, it filled all his body cavities. In *Operation Condor*, he transported several tons back to Hong Kong from the Sahara to make the final shots more authentic.

Everlasting Jade: Coveted treasure in *Half a Loaf of Kung Fu*.

Everybody's Kitchen: Name of Yuen Biao and Jackie's motorized lunch wagon in *Wheels on Meals*.

Evil Valley: Area occupied by renegades in *Magnificent Bodyguards*.

Exchange Rate: 7.747 Hong Kong dollars for one U.S. dollar.

Fairbanks, Douglas: Silent swashbuckler and comedian. A Chan influence.

Farewell My Concubine: Movie starring Gong Li and Leslie Cheung. Closely resembles Chan's childhood.

Film Tech: Jackie's film supply rental company in Hong Kong.

Fire: Element apparent in many Chan movies. In *Crime Story*, he's surrounded by it. In *Police Story II*, he's tortured with it. In *Drunken Master II*, he tortures himself with hot coals.

Fists of Fury: Technique passed on to Jackie in *New Fist of Fury*.

Five Style Technique: Lost style in *Spiritual Kung Fu*.

Foley Artist: Busiest person on a Hong Kong

movie—responsible for putting in the sound effects.

Great White Shark: Jackie's underwater duet partner in *First Strike*.

Gold Dragon: Fan in *Young Master*.

Golden Harvest: Jackie's parent company.

Golden Horse Awards: The Asian film industry awards held in Taiwan.

Golden Way: Jackie's film production company.

Glickenhouse, James: Director of *The Protector*.

Henna: Jackie uses just a bit of this natural dye to add that special red flare to his hair.

HK: Hong Kong.

Holiday: Something Jackie never takes.

Hong Kong Martial Artists Association: Group started by Chan to aid the martial artists of Hong Kong.

Italian Ice Cream: What Jackie's Kowloon office resembles with its many bright colors—lime yellow, bright orange, deep blue, pink and white. The Italian name for the style is *cassata*.

Jackie's Angels: Chan's modeling agency.

Jackie Chan Army: Jackie's stuntmen.

Jackie Chan Charitable Foundation: Organization started by Chan to help needy children.

J.C. Motors: Jackie's car accessories company located in Hong Kong.

Kahn, Michelle (aka Michelle Yeoh): Hong Kong actress and former ballet dancer who gives a marvelous physical performance in *Supercop*. Also appeared in *Project S*.

Keaton, Buster: The physical comedian of silent movies most often mentioned as Jackie's influence.

Kelly, Gene: Chan's model for grace and agility.

Killer Meteor: Flying weapon used by Wang Yu in the movie of the same name.

Kings Gold Medal: An item that when possessed guarantees safe passage through Evil Valley in *Magnificent Bodyguards*.

Kowloon Tong: Location of Jackie's office in Hong Kong. Same area where Bruce Lee had his residence.

Kung hei fat choy: "Happy New Year" in Cantonese.

Lady for a Day: Frank Capra based his movie *Pocketful of Miracles* on this story by Damon Runyon. Jackie in turn based his movie *Miracle* on Capra's work.

Lead Shoes: Training implement used by priests in *Shaolin Wooden Men*.

Lee, Bruce: International action star who met an untimely death under mysterious circumstances. Many tried to make Chan into the "next Bruce Lee." However, he resisted and triumphed with his own style.

Lee Kum Kee: Product featured on billboard that Jackie destroys with his body in *Police Story II*.

Leonard, Sugar Ray: Jackie's second favorite boxer.

Leopard: One of the five animal styles of martial arts. Fierce with poise.

Lion's Roar: Technique used by chained prisoner in *Shaolin Wooden Men*.

Lloyd, Harold: Silent comedian paid homage in *Project A*.

Lo, Kenneth: Jackie's former bodyguard. (See "High-Kicking Lo" sidebar.)

Lo Wei: Director credited with giving Jackie Chan his start in the movies with a string of low-budget actioners. (See "Oh, Why, Lo Wei" sidebar.)

Ma, Dragon: Jackie's character in *Project A*.

Ma, Jingle: Cameraman for many Chan movies.

Macau Grand Prix: Annual car race in Macau.

Man With Six Fingers: Keeper of the Kings Gold Medal in *Magnificent Bodyguards*.

Manga: Japanese comic books. One such book inspired *City Hunter*.

Mars: Chan stuntman and supporting actor. Co-star in *Dragonlord*.

May: Girlfriend in *Police Story*.

Miramax: Movie company. Licensed several of Jackie's older films for stateside release.

Mitsubishi: Japanese car manufacturer that signed Jackie as a spokesperson. Chan's company car, the only one of its kind, is immediately recognizable on the streets of Hong Kong.

Monkey Fares: Name given to costumed dramas, such as *Magnificent Bodyguards*.

Mui, Anita: Singer called the "Madonna of Hong Kong." Also an accomplished actress, appearing in *Drunken Master II* as Chan's stepmother.

My Younger Brother: Tarzan's euphemism for his privates in *Twin Dragons*.

Needham, Hal: Director of *Cannonball Run*.

Neptune Bar: Hangout for criminals in *Police Story II*.

New Line Cinema: American movie company. Licensed several of Jackie's newer movies. *Rumble in the Bronx* was their first release in 1996.

Newman, Paul: American actor Chan most envies because *his* manager doesn't tell *him* he can't race his cars!

NG: Shot not used because of mistakes. NG=No Good.

Norton, Richard: Australian martial artist champion. Regular in Hong Kong movies.

Nose: Part of the body pointed to when Chinese talk in the first person.

Nunchaku: Weapon belonging to the late Bruce Lee's character from *Fists of Fury* that is stolen by Jackie in *New Fist of Fury*.

Ocean Park: Hong Kong version of Disneyland. Where Jackie says he's going at the end of *City Hunter*.

Operation Boarhunt: Mission in *Police Story*.

Pie in the Face: Jackie has often said the only thing he gained from *Battle Creek Brawl* was his English, the ability to roller skate, and an odd penchant for throwing a plate of whipped cream in someone's face on that person's birthday—a tradition he insists is practiced by all people in Texas. He inadvisably taught this little stunt to his martial arts group. "[On my birthday] I just knew that the guys would have the cream waiting for me!" he said. "So I bolted off right after I cut the cake! As a result—no cream on my face! Only disappointment on theirs." Jackie was so enamored of this stunt that some versions of *Police Story* contain a scene at the beginning where police officer Mars is creamed with pie on his birthday. Later in the movie, girlfriend May does the same for Chan.

Pit of Grease: Training forum used by a nun to teach Jackie grace and gentleness in *Shaolin Wooden Men*.

Planet Hollywood: Theme restaurant in which many actors have a share, Chan being one.

Popeye the Sailor Man: Jackie's fighting inspiration in *Fearless Hyena*, complete with spinach.

Presley, Elvis: Late American singer who shares Jackie's trademark smile and high cheekbones.

Reynolds, Burt: Star of *Cannonball Run*.

Ritz, The: Jackie's nightclub in *Miracle*.

Rocky: Jealous boyfriend in *Twin Dragons*.

Rodman, Dennis: Controversial American athlete. Jackie and Jean-Claude Van Damme showed him some kung fu moves in Rome.

"Rose Is Rose": Song sung by Anita Mui in *Miracle* during her impressive costume montage.

Sahara Desert: Filming location for *Operation Condor*.

Samo Hung: Peking Opera school brother. Martial artist in his own right.

Self-Help for the Elderly: Clinic in San Francisco that dedicated an Alzheimer's wing in Jackie's honor in 1996 because of his charitable contributions.

Seven Fist: Technique used by kung fu master in *Spiritual Kung Fu*.

Seven Little Fortunes: Stage name of Jackie and his Peking Opera school brothers.

Shaolin Temple: Ancient Chinese center of Buddhist teaching. Regarded as the birthplace of the martial arts.

Shaw Brothers Studios: Legendary moviemaking studio in Hong Kong where Jackie got his start as an extra. Now they produce only television programs. The studio lot where Jackie made many of his early flicks still exists, however, and he has returned there to film several times, including for *Miracle*, when he knocked down the side of a mountain to make room for one set.

Shing Lung: Translated as "to become a dragon." Lo Wei's name for Jackie.

Shirt: Item costing $2,000 that Jackie ruined by swinging from David Letterman's balcony.

Sideburns: Most obviously fake costume part in *Magnificent Bodyguards*.

Sifu: Title of respect given to a teacher of the martial arts.

Sifu Yu Chan Yuen: The master of the Peking Opera school where Jackie slaved for ten years.

Sleep: What Jackie does on holidays and airplane rides.

Snake: One of the five animal styles of martial arts. Representing mysteries in the heart.

Snake Eye: Informant in *Police Story*.

Sound of Music, The: American musical that Chan claims to have seen sixteen times.

Soul Pearl: Coveted treasure in *Half a Loaf of Kung Fu*.

Stallone, Sylvester: American actor mentioned as a possible costar for Chan. Threw a party for Jackie at Planet Hollywood when *Supercop* premiered in New York, July 1996.

Steel Finger: One of three fake styles. *Half a Loaf of Kung Fu*.

Stewart, Jimmy: Appealing American actor that Jackie's manner resembles in *Miracle*.

Stormy Hills: Location of Evil Valley in *Magnificent Bodyguards*.

Stunt Double: Something Jackie says he doesn't use, although some claim that he does, but only for stunts that might cause him to pop the cork on his patched-up head injury. Even if this is true, what he *does* do is outrageous!

Tang, Edward: Scriptwriter for many Chan movies.

Tarzan: Jackie's buddy in *Twin Dragons*.

Teacups: Always looking for something new and interesting, Jackie latched on to fine porcelain teacups while filming *Rumble in the Bronx* in Vancouver, British Columbia. Apparently one little shop was the object of his interest and he went there several times during filming, amassing hundreds of teacups! They are now proudly displayed in specially designed glass cases throughout his Kowloon office.

Tea House: The bars of the costumed kung fu movie world. Every time Jackie enters one, you can expect a fight.

Tiger: One of the five animal styles of martial arts. Vicious with strength.

Tiger: Jackie's buddy in *Young Master*.

Topps Comics: Publishers of the official Jackie Chan comic book.

Triads: Hong Kong secret societies that plague the movie industry with threats and corruption. Jackie is one of the few Hong Kong actors with enough power to successfully rally against the organized crime influence, helping to create many organizations such as the Directors Guild and Actors Guild to protect Hong Kong talent.

22988: Jackie's prison I.D. in *Island on Fire*.

Undercrank: The process of shooting a scene faster so that the fighters seem quicker. Something that Jackie says he doesn't need.

Underdog: Jackie's character in every movie.

Urquidez, Benny "The Jet": Champion martial artist who goes *mano-a-mano* with Chan in *Wheels on Meals* and *Dragons Forever*.

Walled City: Criminal safe haven in Hong Kong, once a fortress of the Quing Dynasty. Jackie took advantage of the demolition of this cesspool to film explosion scenes for *Crime Story*. A park is now in the Walled City space.

Wash cars: What Jackie sometimes ends up doing on holidays when he's not sleeping. He has more than thirty-two cars, many of them one of a kind.

Water: Water is an elemental theme played out in many Jackie movies.

Drunken Master: Drenched in outdoor vat.
Young Master: Takes a shower.
Project A: Takes a shower.
Police Story: Takes a shower.
Police Story II: May accidentally dumps a bucket of water on Jackie, plus it rains.
Project A II: Thrown into the river.
Twin Dragons: Takes a bubble bath.

Supercop: In the rain.
City Hunter: Ends up in a swimming pool three times.
Drunken Master II: Lau Kar Leung spits on him.

Welles, Orson: Director whose style inspires Jackie in *Miracle*.

"Wherever You Go": Richard Marx song that is one of Chan's favorites.

Whip Hero: Fighter Jackie is mistaken for in *Half a Loaf of Kung Fu*.

White Fan: Gang in *Young Master*.

William Morris Agency: American firm that represents Chan in the United States.

William Tell Overture: Piece conducted by Chan for the Hong Kong Symphony Orchestra after he played a conductor in *Twin Dragons*.

Wine: After making two movies in Australia, *A Nice Guy* and *First Strike*, Jackie became somewhat of an expert on wines. There are many good wineries on the continent. Maybe they were frequented by the crew on days off?

Wong, Oliver: Set designer for many Chan movies, including *First Strike*.

Wooden Men: Mechanical behemoths that Jackie must best at the end of *Shaolin Wooden Men*.

Yuen Biao: Jackie's Peking Opera School brother. Martial artist known for his agility. (See "Bringing Back Biao" sidebar.)

Yugoslavia: Country that was the site of Jackie's most life-threatening accident.

Zatoichi: Famous Japanese swordsman whom Chan parodies at the beginning of *Half a Loaf of Kung Fu*.

IBLIOGRAPHY

Weekly Publications

Brody, James. "In Step with Jackie Chan." *Parade* magazine. 11 Aug. 1996.

Chute, David. "Double Boy." *L.A. Weekly.* 30 Aug. 1991.

Elly, Derek. "More than 'the next Bruce Lee.'" *Variety.* 23–29 Jan. 1995.

Fleming, Michael. "Snipes, Chan say 'Confucius.'" *Variety.* 9 April 1996.

Fleming, Michael. "Chan adds name to 'Smithee.'" *Variety.* 11 Oct. 1996.

Francia, Luis H. "Reel to Reel." *Village Voice.* 1 Sept. 1992.

Gerst, Virginia. "Chan Comes to Chicago." *Diversions.* 28 Feb. 1991.

Hale, James. "Jackie Chan: Asia's No. 1 Movie Star." *Japan Times Weekly.* 5 Aug. 1989.

Hale, James. "Chan Launches New Project." *Japan Times Weekly.* 5 March 1991.

Halligan, Fionnuala. "Film Lovers Tuning In to Hollywood." *South China Morning Post International Weekly.*

Hoberman, J. "Beijing Opera Views." *Village Voice.* 12 May 1992.

Ingram, Bruce. "Hong Kong Fave Chan Making Rare Public Appearance in Chicago." *Variety.* 5 Nov. 1990.

Kehr, Dave. "Chan Can Do." *Film Comment.* May–June 1988.

Kuhn, Eleonare. "The Fall Guy." *Time Out New York*. 21-28 Feb. 1996.

Thompson, Anne. "The Truth About Hits and Dogs." *Entertainment Weekly*. 17 May 1996.

Wolf, Jaime. "Jackie Chan, American Action Hero?" *New York Times Magazine*. 21 Jan. 1996.

Daily Newspapers

Adams, Thelma. "Khan Can like Chan Can in 'Supercop.'" *New York Post*. 26 July 1996.

Barillou, Charles. "Hong Kong's 'Supercops' Thrill With Kung Fu." *The Amsterdam News*. 29 Aug. 1992.

Bernard, Jami. "Alive and Kicking." *New York Post*. 28 Aug. 1992.

Bowles, Scott. "Drunken Master II Shows Chan at his Best." *Dallas Morning News*. 1 Apr. 1994.

Brody, John. "Chan Ready to 'Rumble' in America." *Daily Variety*. 28 Feb. 1995.

Caro, Mark. "Jackie Chan's Mix of Martial Arts and Mirth Wows Crowd." *Chicago Tribune*. 11 Mar. 1991.

Drachman, Steven. "It's 'Westward ho!' for Asian Film Favorite." *Chicago Sun Times*. 24 Feb. 1991.

Halligan, Fionnuala. "Jackie Heading West While Staying East." *South China Morning Post*. 18 Mar. 1995.

Kehr, David. "A Salute to Hong Kong's Daring Cinema." *Chicago Tribune*. 3 Mar. 1991.

Phantom of the Movies. "Kung Fu Fest Is Offering a Chan for all Seasons." *Daily News* (New York). 25 July 1995.

Phantom of the Movies. "Chan's Land of Chop-ortunity." *Daily News* (New York). 19 Feb. 1996.

Vigoda, Arlene. "Jackie Chan gets kick out of singing." *U.S.A. Today*. 16 Aug. 1996.

Worth, Larry. "He Knows Agony of the Feet." *New York Post*. 25 July 1996.

Magazines

Al-Sofi, Joy. Various articles. *The Jackie Chan Fan Club Newsletter*.

Archer, Wayne. "Jackie & I." *Combat.* July 1992.

Author unknown. "Jackie Chan Interview." *Hong Kong Film Connection* (Vol. III, Issue V).

Author unknown. "Stanley Tong: A Talk with Jackie's Favorite Director." *Hong Kong Film Connection* (Vol. III, Issue V).

Author unknown. "Rumble in the Bronx." *World of Fandom.* Spring 1996.

Author unknown. "VIP Lounge." *Premiere.* Oct. 1996.

Booth, Ted. "The Chan Dynasty." *San Francisco International Film Festival Catalogue.* 1989.

Bowman, Diana D. "Jackie Chan Copy One." *The Important Magazine.* Nov. 1994.

Chan, Jackie. Various articles. *Jackie Chan International Fan Club Magazine.*

Chan, Willie. Various articles. *Jackie Chan International Fan Club Magazine.*

Connelly, Bill. Various articles. *Martial Arts Movie Associates.*

Corcoran, John. "City Hunter." *Martial Arts Movies.* March 1993.

Corlis, Richard. "Jackie Can." *Time.* Feb. 1995.

Corlis, Richard. "Asian Invasion." *Time.* Aug. 1995.

Corsello, Andrew. "Chantastic." *GQ.* 1996.

Dannen, Frederic. "Hong Kong Babylon." *New York.* Aug. 1995.

Friedman, Neva. "Jackie Chan Kung Fu Cinema's Newest Sensation." *Playboy.* 1980.

Gentry, Clyde. "Jackie." *Hong Kong Film Connection* (Vol. IV, Issue 1).

Greenfeld, Karl Taro. "Ready to Rumble." *Yolk.* Winter/Spring 1996.

Illavia, Jawaz. "The Battle Plan of Chan the Man." *Impact: The Action Movie Magazine.*

Leeder, Mike. "Jackie Chan Leaping Into Action." *Eastern Heroes* (Issue #10).

Little, John. "Ken Lo: Stepping Out of Jackie's Shadow." *Inside Kung Fu.* Sept. 1996.

Long, Nathan. "Chinese Fix." *Film Threat Video Guide.*

Logan, Bey. "The Jackie Chan Interview." *Martial Arts Illustrated.*

Logan, Bey. "Jackie Chan Interview." *Impact: The Action Movie Magazine.*

Logan, Bey. "Jackie Chan: The Dragon Rising." *Combat.* March 1988.

May, Don E. "Jackie Chan Stuntfest Spectacular." *Film Threat.* June 1994.

Meyers, Ric. "Taste the International Flavor." *Inside Kung-Fu.* March 1991.

Meyers, Ric. "Team Chan USA Comes to the Rescue." *Inside Kung-Fu.* May 1996.

Miller, Ricky, and Joey O'Bryan. "Chan Interview." *Hong Kong Film Connection* (Vol. IV, Issue 1).

Rascon, Catherine. "Jackie Chan: Les Kids de Hong Kong." *Hors Seni Cinema*.

Rawcliffe, Shaun. "Jackie Chan: The Man Behind the Image." *Combat*. Feb. 1992.

Reid, Dr. Craig D. "An Evening With Jackie Chan." *Bright Lights*. 1994.

Rhodes, Scott. "The 25 Greatest Stunts of All Time." *Action Films*. Nov. 1992.

Vie, Caroline. "The Jackie Chan Interview." *Inside Kung-Fu*. 1995.

Witterstaetter, Renée. "The Name Is Chan: Jackie Chan." *Return to Jurassic Park* (Comic #9). Topps Comics. Feb. 1996.

Yu Mo Wan. "The Kwan Tak Hing Era." *Hong Kong Film Magazine*. (Issue #2). 1994.

Yu Mo Wan. "Who Was the Real Wong Fei Hong?" *Hong Kong Film Magazine* (Issue #2). 1994.

Books

Logan, Bey. *Hong Kong Action Movies* (First Edition). New York: Overlook Press, 1996.

McGregor, Don. *Buster Keaton: The Early Years* (First Edition). Staten Island, NY: Eclipse Enterprises, 1982.

Meyers, Richard, Amy Harlib, Bill and Karen Palmer. *From Bruce Lee to the Ninjas: Martial Arts Movies* (First Edition). New York: Citadel Press, 1985.

I'd also like to acknowledge others who have written about Jackie Chan and Hong Kong cinema, including the following: Alex Jay, Keith Bearden, Georgia Brown, Steven Drachman, David Everitt, Ted D. Fishman, Michael Glitz, Sue Green, Chris Hicks, Steve Jones, Mark LaSalle, John Leicester, Patrick Z. McGavin, Josh Rottenberg, Matt Zoller Seitz, Henry Sheehan, Margaret Sheridan, Neil Strauss, Nathaniel Wice and Norman Yam.